Transformational Decade

*Snapshots of a Decade
from 9/11 to the Obama Presidency*

Herbert I. London

Hamilton Books
an imprint of
University Press of America,® Inc.
Lanham · Boulder · New York · Toronto · Plymouth, UK

Copyright © 2012 by
Hamilton Books
4501 Forbes Boulevard
Suite 200
Lanham, Maryland 20706
UPA Acquisitions Department (301) 459-3366

Estover Road
Plymouth PL6 7PY
United Kingdom

First paperback edition 2013

All rights reserved

British Library Cataloging in Publication Information Available

The hardback edition of this book was previously catalogued by the Library of Congress as follows:

Library of Congress Control Number: 2012937342
ISBN: 978-0-7618-5908-6 (clothbound)
ISBN: 978-0-7618-6159-1 (pbk.)
ISBN: 978-0-7618-5909-3 (electronic)

*To my wife Vicki and my three daughters,
Stacy, Nancy and Jaclyn*

Contents

Introduction	7
Chapter 1 America Agoniste	13
Chapter 2 The Age of Experimentation	31
Chapter 3 The Slippery Slope of Cultural Degradation	52
Chapter 4 False Prophets	68
Chapter 5 Technology Is Creating A Brave or Foolish New World	80
Chapter 6 The End of Bipartisanship	91
Chapter 7 Ignorance Is Not Bliss	112
Chapter 8 Things Fall Apart	138
Epilogue	161
Endnotes	165
Index	169

Introduction

Decades, to some degree, are defined by events. They are bounded by extraordinary conditions, rather than chronology. The year 2000 was seemingly benign as the world focused on the anniversary of the millennium. Violent events in Saudi Arabia, Yemen, and East Africa served as a foreshadowing of the future, but President Clinton assumed terrorism promoted among Muslims could be controlled through police action. After all, with the exception of the first attack on the World Trade Center, these events in the 1990s were in far away distant lands.

"What me worry?" was a national refrain even though Muslims intent on engendering destruction made it clear they had declared war on the United States, "the Great Satan." The Dow Jones average was approaching 12,000 and youngsters on Wall Street were paying cash for multimillion dollar apartments in Manhattan. All was not right with the world, but for an instant it looked pretty good. Alas, it was only an instant. In the presidential campaign of 2000, neither Al Gore nor George Bush stressed foreign policy. In fact, with reference to the first Gulf War and maintenance of "the no fly zone" the soon-to-be President Bush said we should not be engaged in nation building in Iraq or anywhere else. History would soon intrude on this claim.

On September 11, 2001, the world changed. The attack on the World Trade Center and the Pentagon took almost 3000 lives, more than those killed at Pearl Harbor seventy years earlier. It wasn't as if Islamic terrorism was unknown; what shattered the national psyche was the extent to which America is vulnerable to attack. The "far away" reached our shores. When it did, forces were put into play that were not previously contemplated.

There may have been a war against the United States, but it was not a war we engaged until 9/11. From that moment to this, U.S. forces have been deployed across the Middle East to Afghanistan in an effort to "clear the swamp" of terrorists and prevent another attack within our borders. Many have questioned this strategy and many are suffering from war fatigue, yet it is true that despite plans and efforts by Islamists, another successful attack against the United States has not occurred.

We have, however, paid for this war in blood and treasure. It has also had a profound effect on national sentiments. Soon after 9/11 the nation was united, galvanized by the attack with expressions of patriotic fervor. In time, however, that unity evanesced, replaced by skepticism, even cynicism. Those with a conspiratorial bent argued the CIA or Mossad or some sinister group was really behind the 9/11 attack. Others argued the war in Iraq wasn't justified because Iraq wasn't behind the 9/11 attack, and the Colin Powell argument that the war was necessary to thwart Iraq's nuclear weapons program, proved to be erroneous.

If the attack on the United States united Americans, the body bags of G.I.'s unraveled national unity. Americans have seemingly lost the will for an attenuated war; however, this will be a long war fought on many fronts with a shadowy enemy inspired by religious doctrine and imperial ambitions. We may want this bloodshed to end, but as one Salafist leader noted, "You love life, we love death. That is our advantage."

In what can only be characterized as a replay of the Cold War, many Americans turned on themselves arguing that security should not jeopardize civil liberties. During the Cold War there were communists, anti-communists, and anti-anti-comunists. The latter group was far more concerned with the threat of Joseph McCarthy than Joseph Stalin. Now there are terrorists, anti-terrorists, and anti-anti-terrorists. In this instance the anti-anti-terrorists are preoccupied with George W. Bush, the Patriot Act, and CIA tactics rather than the threat of al Qaeda and various terrorist organizations.

It is curious that 9/11 opened the Pandora's Box of the freedom-security equation with waterboarding as a tactic for securing vital intelligence the gravamen of ideological tension. For many, President Bush and his strategy at home and abroad for keeping Americans safe from another attack became the concern. Rather than offer credit for a remarkable safety record since 9/11, Bush was often characterized as an extremist overreaching to terrorism's influence. This, of course, is a little like proving a null hypothesis: Was America safe because of actions taken by the president or safe because the threat was overstated? Because I believe the former, the outpouring of anti-Bush/Cheney sentiment, which became a torrent near the end of the decade, was disheartening.

It was also apparent that the nation, told to return to normalcy, was living beyond its means, borrowing capriciously against the future. To cite one example, the Community Reinvestment Act in the mid-1980s used government-subsidized mortgages to create the illusion that everyone could own a home, notwithstanding their present financial condition. When redlining was made a felony, banks could not apply green-eye-shade logic to lending programs. Although this factor did not lead directly to the credit meltdown of 2008, it was a contributing condition. Wall Street had to contend with greed, but the nation has to deal with unrealistic spending and an unfunded liability approaching six to seven times gross domestic product.

Despite Cassandras who presaged a recession or perhaps worse—a depression—members of both parties averted their gaze believing that the country could muddle through the difficult times. Sacrifice was not a word Americans suitably employed. In fact, Americans had been seduced by government hand-outs never asking who will pay the piper. The blame game began in earnest when it finally dawned on most citizens that the financial system was in disarray; however, most people refused to look at themselves in a mirror.

I believe that it would be a mistake to underestimate the resilience of Americans; however, it is also true that the national spirit suffered a devastating blow with attacks from without and a loss of confidence from within. One manifestation of this uneasiness was the rise of declinism, a Spenglerian belief that the West (read: United States) is in decline. One book after another argued that America's global hegemony was over, historical events and conditions conspired to end exceptionalism. For proponents of this position, America was like any other nation with a distinctive past, but certainly no better or worse.

It was hardly coincidental that those who embraced this view contended that the future was inextricably linked to transnational progressivism, a belief that sovereignty must be relinquished for international organizations and authority. The United States would serve as a member in good standing of the emerging international community, one with linkages that go beyond the United Nations.

These tendencies in American life emerged full blown with the presidential campaign of 2008. Although Barack Obama campaigned as a centrist, who was "beyond race," his background and associations suggested he is a man of the hard left, the kind of man American's generally reject; however, the anti-Bush sentiment, along with a downturn in the economy and a press effort to undermine the war effort, came together as a political tsunami for the youthful candidate, yielding an unprecedented presidential victory.

Most assumed, despite his background, that President Obama would govern as he campaigned, but that would be wrong. In the first year of his presidency, Barack Obama opted to reinvent America, to alter its position on every major issue. The year 2009 was the culminating boundary in the decade, what can only be described as a transformational moment.

Who would have guessed that in a mere several months the federal government would have an ownership in the financial services industry, banking, insurance, automobile manufacturing, and healthcare. The free market itself has been imperiled by the overreaching of an administration intent on "spreading the wealth." President Obama has chosen to govern America as if he were a European Social Democrat, making even FDR and LBJ appear as fiscal moderates. The inspiration for the excessive spending is the ghost of John Maynard Keynes, who did, under limited circumstances, argue for government stimulus in a recessionary cycle. The Obama team was actually Keynes on steroids.

The spending and stimulus activity paled in significance to the initiatives in foreign policy. Whenever there was occasion to do so, President Obama apologized for actions in America's past. These apologies insulted the memory of those whose graves litter the European continent so that prosperity and freedom could emerge. The appeal for forgiveness campaign has gone on unabated, now joined by the effort to downgrade America's international role outside the confines of the United Nations.

On top of that President Obama has done whatever he could to blemish the reputation of former President George Bush, including but not restricted to the trial of Khalid Sheikh Mohammed in a civilian court so that the anti-terrorist methods of the Bush years will be fully disclosed, thereby satisfying the bloodlust of anti-anti-terrorists who hate Bush more than Osama bin Laden.

This is apiece with a foreign policy that relies on appeasement, more accurately preemptive conciliation. President Obama has shown a willingness to concede to such enemies as Iran and deal harshly with such allies as Israel. The reinvention of America does not stop at our shores. The president apparently wants to increase foreign aid without regard to reciprocal gestures. "Spread the wealth" means more than simply domestic redistribution of resources.

The question that remains is whether Americans, even those that voted for President Obama, bargained for change this dramatic. It is not as if historical forces are moving America in this global direction. As Charles Krauthammer has noted, "declinism is a choice." Alas, when the president noted, "you (his constituents) are the change we have been waiting for," few recognized this as revolutionary change different from American principles.

Yet here we are, a new decade in a new century, with a set of new ideas different from any Americans have seen before. This president wants to railroad them through before careful examination occurs (vide: the 1900-page Stimulus Bill submitted the day before a vote).

Frederick Lewis Allen wrote two decade analyses, *Only Yesterday and Since Yesterday*, which characterized the 1920s and the 1930s, respectively. If I had to characterize this decade between 9/11 and the Obama presidency, I would call it "Post Yesterday," a period that breaks with the past, that socializes a free market economy, and that diminishes America's standing on the world stage. This is transformational America that the following pages will describe through snapshots of the recent past. It is not a history, but rather a peek through the lens of various events. It is neither encyclopedic nor narrowly chronological, but the articles in the aggregate present a tale of a new thematic America unfolding before our very eyes.

Whether the people will ultimately accept what the president offers remains to be seen, but the America on September 10, 2001, looks vastly different from the America in January 2010, and, from my perch, the direction is not desirable. Nonetheless, as an American cultivated with a belief in guarded optimism, I hope for the best and will marshal my energies to work for the best as well.

On another level, "the end of history" (to cite Francis Fukuyama's title) looks very much like the beginning. Conflicts abound, and despite President Obama conciliatory approach, enemies haven't mitigated their hatred of the United States. Perhaps this is a positive sign that may force President Obama to abandon utopian ideas and embrace realistic perspectives; however, here, too, the jury is out awaiting the decisions of the next decade.

Chapter 1
America Agoniste

The United States of today is a long way away from the values and principles on which the nation was founded. Can we recover and renew those values for today?

In Edward Bellamy's novel *Looking Backward*[1], the principal character was mesmerized and put to sleep for decades. When he awakened, the world had changed; the socialist impulses of Bellamy and his technological predictions (quite accurate it turned out) were very much on display. It was most noteworthy that individual aspirations had been converted into collective designs; wealth had spread and new forms of technology littered the landscape.

Although I found myself disagreeing with much of Bellamy's philosophical disposition, it struck me that the exercise of looking back is a useful one. For example, suppose I had been mesmerized in 1965 and awakened in 2010. How might the nation appear to a pilgrim who had been asleep for more than four decades?

For one thing, I might ask if I live in America. The civil rights legislation of the 1960s was predicated on the idea that race and ethnicity should be neither a handicap nor an asset in public life. In 2010, by contrast, Ms. Sonia Sotomayor, despite a lackluster record as a judge, was confirmed as a Supreme Court justice because of her Hispanic background and her "empathetic" experience with the poor and downtrodden.

In the 1960s it was clear (despite growing cynicism) that the United States was founded on Judeo-Christian principles. Our founders recognized the nexus between biblical prescriptions and political institutions. By 2010 America has become a nation that has deracinated the Judeo-Christian tradition from public life. In fact, President Obama said the United States is one of the largest Muslim nations in the world even though roughly 3 million Muslims live in this nation of 320 million people.

In the 1960s SDS and many anti-Vietnam supporters marched in candlelight vigils to protest the war in Vietnam, but despite hardcore radicals most Americans and certainly most legislators supported their country. By 2010 a substantial number of Americans want to see the United States lose a war in Iraq and be forced into an ignominious surrender in the Middle East.

In the 1960s General Motors was the world's largest car manufacturer and a company that stood as an example of the nation's economic strength. In 2010 G.M. is in bankruptcy, more than 60 percent of the company is owned by the government, and half of its brands have been removed from the market. Moreover, the nation's free market-described by Europeans pejoratively as Anglo-Saxon capitalism-has now been replaced by the command economy with Washington largely in control of the means of production. Eighty percent of American International Group is now owned by the federal government; 30 percent of Citicorp is in the same position; federal authorities imposed a merger on the Chrysler Corporation, and, if President Obama has his way, health care representing 17 percent of the economy will also be controlled by the federal government.

In 1963 American students reached the apogee on SAT tests and international exams in science and math vis-à-vis foreign competitors. By 2010 the U.S. students scored near the bottom in these international tests, notwithstanding an enormous increase in educational spending in the last four decades.

There are days when I think it would be best if I could remain asleep in 1965. The nation was somewhat innocent, as was I. Socialism was a concept mocked here and abroad, and even in the Soviet Union by homegrown intellectuals. The United States was a hegemon on the world stage, often criticized, but also recognized as a world power. It was inconceivable that any president, in the presence of world leaders, would apologize for the transgressions in American foreign policy.

Race was being subordinated as a concept for employment and college admission in the 1960s, despite the Jim Crow legacy of the past. God was in his heaven and much was right in the world.

Now I question whether the America of 2010 is American at all. Is this merely an aberrational moment or are we headed down a new and a dangerous direction, one inconsistent with our traditions and principles?

Perhaps someone will wake me from this disturbing dream and say, *yes*, America is well and still the land of the free; however, I've come to learn that being mesmerized can be very discomforting.

It is natural for anyone older than 60 to grow nostalgic with the passage of time. After all, where did that time go and why so quickly? There is another issue, that comes with advanced years, and that is the extent and acceleration of change.

When most commentators discuss change they invariably mean such technical developments as computerization, cell phones, fax machines, and supersonic jets that have profoundly changed our lives. On the other hand, I am far more startled by cultural change (i.e., how we live and speak to one another, and the gap that emerges in generational views).

I read an article in *The Country Chronicle* that corresponds to my own confusion with the present time. For example, when I grew up, "gay" meant you were happy; people cut grass-they didn't smoke it-and my mother used "pot" to boil noodles.

I can remember when men didn't hug and women didn't curse. Baseball players didn't do a little dance around home plate when they hit a home run and basketball players didn't preen in front of a television camera after a dunk.

I was once obliged to call older folks "Sir and Ma'am," and had to cover my mouth when I coughed. I could never eat outdoors unless it was at a picnic or a hot dog stand. If my gum wrapper fell outside the perimeter of a garbage container, I felt guilty if I didn't pick it up.

Yes, that was many years ago. In fact, it was so long ago that people actually took responsibility for their actions. Who would have thought of suing the government if you fell down and broke a leg in a public facility?

There was a moment when "time sharing" meant getting together with the family and "quality time" meant a walk with mom or dad. If a friend asked if I "made out," he usually meant did I pass the exam. Kids routinely went to the movies for excitement, not titillation.

When I played basketball, the last thing you would do on the court is embarrass an opponent. On report cards, most teachers believed God gets an A, teachers get a B, and students get what's left-if they work for it. Senior year in high school was not a time for trips and public service-classes were held and students were expected to attend. How quaint!

If someone told me right and wrong are relative, I would have introduced him to my uncles who fought in World War II. The ensuing conversation would be very brief. A "home entertainment unit" was a family sing, "hard rock" was redundant, and "scoring" was solely related to points on the basketball court.

I have a difficult time with "assisted living" as a concept because I assume it's an old person using a cane. I similarly don't know when the middle years reached the sixties and adolescence ended at thirty.

Food tastes have certainly changed. I can remember when pasta was spaghetti and coffee didn't have foam at the top of it. When I went to a restaurant no one ever asked me how I liked my fish cooked. Moreover, I still don't know why anyone eats uncooked fish, albeit that's th e only way my daughters like it.

Courtship is yet another antediluvian idea, a distant cousin of bar hopping. If someone talked about "hooking up" it meant installing a shower curtain in the bathroom. "Getting to first base" meant hitting a single. Sex and the single girl were oxymoronic, except, of course, for the fast girls who didn't remain single very long. A "pill" was a dull person, but he didn't prevent pregnancy. People lived together, but they generally got married first. Wives needed husbands to have babies.

Rap was something you did when the doorbell didn't ring. Hanging out was what you put on the line to dry. Cool was the way you drank lemonade and a "hottie" was my mother's chicken soup.

A navel was never exposed, tattoos were for sailors exclusively, and basketball players wore shorts, not short long pants. "Dis" was a sound made by angry cats. Hip-hop was something you did when you played potzie on the streets.

There was a time when .240 hitters didn't make it to the majors, much less get million dollar contracts. Men had hair on their chests and women didn't have hair under their arms. If asked, "where have you gone Joe DiMaggio?" the answer was center field.

All was not right with this world of my past. There were wars and poverty, racial conflict, and recession, but I was less confused. Yes, there has always been a generation gap, but now it's a valley and I'm afraid it's too wide to cross. What I hope for is a cycle with some return to the culture I best remember. Anyone for charlotte russe?

The past is unfortunately a distant memory, and the language of the past has been obscured by the confusion in the present.

George Orwell's contribution to contemporary media communication is undeniable. Orwellian logic (e.g. "war is peace") is ensconced in almost every news broadcast.

When riots occurred in Cincinnati after an unarmed felon was shot by a police officer, news accounts invariably referred to "protesters on the streets"; either; however, these "protesters" who broke into stores, stole property, and arbitrarily beat and abused passersby should have been called what they are (i.e., thugs or criminals or miscreants). "Protesters" merely denies the reality.

It is also the case that Jesse Jackson and Al Sharpton are always cited as "civil rights leaders." Based on recent revelations about the financial legerdemain in Jackson's for-profit and not-for-profit empire and the proposed boycott of Burger King by Sharpton's minions, it would be consistent with the truth to call these men extortionists or shake-down artists. Surely lining their own pockets is not a civil right.

Another of the terms now virtually a mantra on university campuses is "diversity"; diversity as presently employed refers only to skin color. Having blacks or browns on campus constitutes diversity. The one condition universities will not tolerate is diversity of opinion. A variety of diverse views on race, for example, is a violation of the newly constituted diversity standard.

"Multiculturalism" similarly means anything but many cultures. In fact, its central and overarching concern is antipathy to anything American. If truth in advertising prevailed, then "multiculturalism" would be uniculturalism.

A recent study indicated that "child care centers" do not duplicate the level of concern and care offered by moms. Although this study may present self-evident conclusions, it has not influenced the use of labels. It would seem that an appropriate name for "child care centers" should be "alternative care centers." The title may not appeal to feminists who believe that mom is better placed in a job than at home with infants. Some feminists may need the illusion child care is going on in the centers where kids are deposited.

On the foreign policy front Secretary of State Colin Powell contends that Israel's reaction to violence should be "neither excessive nor disproportionate." The translation of this when two fourteen year olds are stoned to death for no other reason except their Jewishness remains unclear. Moreover, Powell is the author of a doctrine that demands overwhelming military force to subdue an enemy, as was the case in the Gulf War. Perhaps what the secretary means is the United States should employ overwhelming force when it is at war, but our allies must respond to violence "proportionately."

Another term that has always perplexed me is the "Internal Revenue Service." To whom, I wonder, is a service provided? It would be far more accurate to call this government department R.C.T. (Revenue Coerced from Taxpayers.) Keep in mind that someone bringing a meal to your restaurant table offers a service; collecting revenue from an unwilling taxpayer is coercion.

Why, one might well ask, have these Orwellianisms entered our vocabulary and why do media moguls use them with regularity? Part two obviously answers part one. Media use helps to explain public use.

From the standpoint of the guardians of news and views there is an implicit desire to influence, to shape opinion about events. One is more inclined to accept the views of "protesters" rather than "renegades."

A civil rights leader is more acceptable as a public figure than a shakedown artist. Multicultural is more acceptable than anti-American. Proportionate military responses seem more morally acceptable than disproportionate reaction.

As a consequence, turning words on their head, offering meaning unintended by the word's origin, influences opinion. There are several tests of this contention that are infallible.

When someone describes a position as "humanitarian," that really means the speaker thinks his or her view is better than yours. More often than not, there is nothing humanitarian about it. When someone says the issue is "more complicated than you think," that person really means your position is wrong, not "complicated."

Some might contend these word games are innocuous. So what if the *New York Times*, for example, calls thugs "protesters." I maintain words are ideas incarnate. If words are used inaccurately, thoughts cannot be accurate. In *1984* Orwell argued that a venal government changed the meaning of a word for its own purpose. One can only wonder why it is happening now. Words are also evocative. Embedded in them are ideas, history, and culture. The evolution of words, how they can assume the opposite of their initial intent or, for that matter, lose meaning altogether, is most interesting. Let me cite several illustrations.

Most Americans contend they live in a democracy (i.e. government by the people). As students of politics know, however, the people do not rule directly, but rather, through their representatives, which, of course, makes the United States a republic.

It is hypocritical to pretend to be what one is not. As La Rochefoucauld noted, "hypocrisy is the tribute vice pays virtue." The impairment of virtue, however, should be labeled accurately (i.e., corruption).

On the hypocrisy front, the word *liberal* has undergone a complete transformation. "Liberal" once meant broadminded, tolerant, and not bound by orthodoxy; if one considers its present usage, it is invariably intolerant of other opinions and devoted to an orthodoxy of big government and an intrusive command economy.

Two words in current parlance are used interchangeably: authoritarian and totalitarian regimes; however, each word has refinements that are meaningful. Authoritarian regimes are those that favor the concentration of power in a leader or an elite. Totalitarian regimes regulate and control every aspect of the life and productive capacity of the nation. As former ambassador to the United Nations, Jeane Kirkpatrick[2], among others, noted that in authoritarian states the concentration of power may leave some dimension of uncontrolled private life with the citizenry (e.g. religion). By contrast, totalitarian regimes control every dimension of life.

Some words simply lose vitality because they cannot keep up with the acceleration of events. Pornography, for example, meant the depiction of erotic behavior intended to cause sexual excitement; however, the sting in the word is lost when it appears everywhere.

A sister of pornography, the word *obscene* has had a similar fate. The word meaning abhorrent to morality or virtue, that which is designed to incite lust or depravity, has fallen into desuetude in large part because what was once readily considered obscene is now observed during primetime television viewing hours. To even suggest a given condition is obscene places one in the position of a prude, a fate comparable to a Puritanical attitude.

To censor or supervise conduct and morals and delete objectionable matter has similarly been converted into a synonym for repression. When former Mayor Rudolph Giuliani established a decency committee to assess the expenditure of public funds on the arts, talk show host Jay Leno described him a "fascist." It is interesting that the word *society*, meaning the pursuit of common interest and standards by an association of people, implies a standard for the expenditure of public funds.

The word artist has clearly evolved from a person skilled in painting, music, sculpture, writing, and the like into a *soi disant* characteristic. If funding for the arts is available, many people will call themselves artists even if the skill, training, and practice in the arts aren't evident.

That brings me to another word whose meaning has been clouded by relativistic assertions. The word *principle* is a basic truth or, at least, was a basic truth involving a fixed moral and ethical standard; however, in a society where standards are in flux-where one person's standard is another person's preference-principle has been a casualty.

I do not believe that vocabulary is entirely fixed; however, it should be noted that if words do not have a reliable meaning, then neither do thoughts or the power to reason. Words are ideas incarnate. To subject them to the whims of the user is to increase the propensity for anarchy, a state of disorder and lawlessness.

Perhaps in the *Alice in Wonderland* world in which we live words can mean whatever you want them to mean. Some people may actually like that idea; however, if you want to avoid totalitarianism and uphold principle, it's a good idea that words convey precisely what you have in mind.

When asked to describe the goal of the Constitutional Convention Ben Franklin said, "A Republic, if you can keep it." The last five words are critical. For in the succeeding two hundred years the Republic has undergone shifts and dramatic changes. It is certain that the limited government envisioned by the founders does not resemble the government of today that by happenstance, pandering, or addressing real and perceived needs is elephantine.

Perhaps the most significant challenge to a republican form of government is the liberal state that emphasizes rights as its critical feature. Rights tend to be inviolable; moreover, a privilege vouchsafed over several months morphs easily into a right.

Rent control in New York City, for example, proffered as a temporary measure to assist G.I.'s returning from World War II, was transmogrified into a right that doesn't make economic sense and certainly has little application to the city 60 years after its introduction.

The liberal state is fond of finding and then defending rights the founders could not possibly have imagined. Reproductive rights, the right to healthcare, and the right to marry a member of the same sex are clearly contemporary rights that come to mind.

The problem with newly created rights is that they take on a status like those in the Bill of Rights; they must be defended and applied as if the First Amendment. There is no end to their invention and metamorphosis from idea to privilege to right.

Rights are also universal; they apply to those who pay taxes and those who don't; they apply to new immigrants and the old; they may even be applied to those who arrive on our shores illegally. Hence, rights can fundamentally alter the character of a nation, even as we take pride in many rights (e.g., individual rights, property rights) as being essential for the continued qualities in our nation.

Republicanism is summarized in three words, "we the people." Our Constitution does not refer to "we the states" or to "a polity." The government presumably serves the will of the people and acts on the consent of the governed; therefore, rights must be seen against a backdrop of consent. If the people are willing to abjure some rights in order to enhance security, that is their privilege.

Liberalism has so encroached on the essence of the Republic that the courts have arrogated to themselves the right to make laws the Constitution earmarked for Congress. This has occurred without much of an outcry from the public.

Thus, the reason for the failure of the recent immigration bill is that the proposed legislation represented liberal overreaching. By suggesting people who violated American sovereignty should be rewarded with the rights of citizens struck those with a republican orientation as absurd. This was seen, rightly or wrongly, as the frivolous dissemination of rights.

The proliferation of rights is not accompanied by a devotion to duties. People assume rights are manufactured-as indeed they often are-and are served to the American people cost free. As a consequence, there is a natural constituency for rights proliferation and not one for a traditional republican form of government.

There are many areas of public life where the consent of the governed should prevail. If the public is wary of radical Islam and its penchant for violence, must we say rights should be applied to radical Muslims and Muslims alike? If the people are unwilling to embrace guest workers who do not have any interest in being American-speaking our language, learning our customs and history, and sacrificing for the nation-does it make sense to extend the rights of American citizens to these workers?

The tension between the liberalism of John Stuart Mill and the republicanism of Jefferson is clearly embedded in our history. In a sense, this moment is not different from others; however, we have tilted so far in a liberal direction that we have lost our way. It's time to rebalance philosophical assumptions and restore consent of the governed into the national debate on public policy issues.

In 1787 a Scottish history professor at the University of Edinburgh, Alexander Tyler[3], writing about the fall of the Athenian Republic some 2000 years ago, argued that democracy is always temporary in nature. He maintained that at some point a majority will discover that it can vote itself generous emoluments from the public treasury and, in keeping with this theme, support the candidates who promise the most benefits. At some point, he contends, democracy collapses due to a debased fiscal policy and is replaced by a dictatorship.

Tyler clearly wasn't alone in his assessment of democracy because Plato voiced the same concern soon after the fall of the Athenian Republic. Self-aggrandizement in the sense of getting something from the labors of someone else is an inherent weakness in democratic organization.

From Toynbee to Sorokin, from Tyler to Spengler[4], historians of civilization have addressed the patterns that account for the rise and fall of various governments. Toynbee contends that civilizations over time lose their will and fervor to survive; Sorokin argues that sensate considerations trump ideational values turning societies into pleasure-seeking entities that cannot sustain themselves, and, for Spengler, will is diminished by a loss of belief and confidence in the political organization leading ultimately to decline.

Tyler believes that "the average age of the world's greatest civilizations from beginning of history, has been about 200 years. During those 200 years, these nations always progressed through the following sequence: From bondage to spiritual faith; from spiritual faith to great courage;

from courage to liberty; from liberty to abundance; from abundance to complacency; from complacency to apathy; from apathy to dependence; from dependence back into bondage.

Anyone reading this analysis will surely see some parallels to our own democracy. Close to half of the American people do not pay personal income tax yet are increasingly insistent that those who do provide them with ever larger benefits (i.e., in healthcare and retirement care).

The courage displayed by our founding fathers in defying British overlords and establishing a Constitution has transmuted into complacency; some might call it living off the fat of the land. So many Americans are dependent on government-in one way or another-to address their needs that the first question interrogators ask presidential candidates is invariably, "what will your election do for me?"

Moreover, the question many foreign governments ask of the United States is if you are having a hard time sustaining your democracy because of intrinsic flaws, why do you assume it is a form of government desirable for our people? Democracy clearly can establish stability and as clearly, relying on the will of the people is more desirable than reliance on a leader, however benign; but, there are dependency characteristics that offer concern.

Is the Tyler scenario formulaic? Can democracies forestall this pattern? History, of course, is replete with idiosyncratic examples. It is also true, that the evolution Tyler depicts has the ring of truth and enough empirical evidence to warrant self-examination.

The road to political success is paved with promises. Those who promise more are usually the victors. With these promises a consensus emerges. Could any politician in the United States today, for example, rail against Social Security or Medicare? Could they say that these legislative entities have an unfunded liability six times the G.D.P.? The public wouldn't stand for these comments even if true. People want "what is coming to them."

John Kettle, a seventeenth-century English philosopher, wrote: "Any time any opinion comes to be held by nearly everyone, it is nearly always wrong." Kettle was right, but "wrong" in this matter is a normative judgment. In democracy the people speak and that opinion will prevail, even if a majority is wrong. This is a flaw democracies must overcome or perish.

Alexander Tyler did not live to see modern democracy; however, it is fair to postulate that what he said may afflict democracies, and may indeed be afflicting us now. History, of course, waits in judgment. That is a judgment, however, we should wisely seek to influence.

At the moment, the nature of our democracy and its future direction are in question, which prompts the question: Where do I live? Until the Supreme Court decisions in *Grutter* and *Gratz* and the *Lawrence* case[5], I thought my home was the United States. After all, I pledged my allegiance to America, sang "The Star Spangled Banner" with brio, and read the Declaration of Independence and the Constitution to remind myself of the nation's founding.

Now I believe I might be living in Malaysia or perhaps a South American country like Brazil. I'm confused. The principles I associated with the United States have been discarded by the Supreme Court in so cavalier a manner that this nation I love seems to have been transformed into a banana republic.

Take two fundamental ideas that served as a foundation stone for the national edifice: equal protection under the law and the precepts of a Judeo-Christian society. With the Supreme Court decisions in question these principles have been shredded into confetti.

"Equal protection" once suggested, as the Fourteenth Amendment noted and the Civil Rights act of 1964 reaffirmed, that no one should be handicapped nor advantaged by virtue of race. This was the idea behind the integration of races and what civil rights advocates fought for from the Civil War through the 1960s.

Notwithstanding all the claims to the contrary, from the 1970s on "equal opportunity" became confused with "equal results." A nation that often saw its principles honored in the breach decided to overturn the principle and employ race as a proxy for the "disadvantaged."

Thus was born the era of affirmative action. In this new age, diversity meant only racial diversity. As a consequence, admissions' officers in universities counted by race, denying along the way that this wasn't a quota system.

Even though the Supreme Court's *Bakke* decision in the late 1970s said race could be used as one criterion for admission, state courts argued that race was an inappropriate criterion unless there was prior evidence of overt discrimination. In *Grutter* and *Gratz* race is officially valorized; it is the criterion for admission even though a weighted numerical standard for race was found unacceptable.

In the majority opinion written by Sandra Day O'Connor, the equal protection clause is officially negated, ascriptive standards of the kind reproved by the nation's founders are embraced. Instead of being the beacon of fair play America has been Latin Americanized through designated privilege.

The *Lawrence* decision may have even more insidious characteristics than *Gratz* and *Gutter*. In this decision state sodomy laws were reversed. This is a position with which I'm in accord. The Court, however, didn't stop there. It permanently ensconced "the privacy notion" mentioned in the *Griswold* decision and *Roe v. Wade*, but certainly not found in the Constitution. This is law by invention.

Moreover, the law now created reverses 2000 years of Judeo-Christian tradition because a majority of the Court contends what is done in the privacy of one's bedroom is no one's business except the participants. In other words, incest, prostitution, adultery, or any other perversion the mind can conjure cannot be regulated. Morality is now officially an individual concern unrelated to social responsibility or biblical prescription.

The liberal idea has been transmogrified into the libertine ideal. "Go where you want to go, do what you want to do," the refrain of Woodstock generation, is the decisive position of the Supreme Court. It is remarkable that in a scant three decades 2000 years of tradition have been discarded. Sodom and Gomorrah are no longer an object lesson; they are sanctified in official fabricated legal theory.

I am indeed confused about where I live. Never did I think that principles as fundamental as "equal protection" and regulation against taboos could so easily be rejected. This is not the America I signed on to, nor is it the America our founders created.

In my judgment the Supreme Court has lost its way and it is taking the nation with it. Legal precedent and common sense have all gone down the rabbit's hole. All someone with my view can hope for is that someday-hopefully before the twenty-five years when Sandra Day O'Connor indicated affirmative action should end-the nation will reclaim its heritage and recall what made America an exceptional nation and the hope for people in every corner of the globe.

Of course, it is not only the Supreme Court that has lost its way.

On both the left and the right in the United States "diversity" is a word transmogrified into policy. The left contends that designated groups discriminated against in the past should be given preferential treatment in the present. By contrast, the right contends that diversity should be more than counting by skin color or ethnicity. It argues that first and foremost universities, obsessed with diversity, should promote diversity of ideas.

In sum, we as Americans face a society exploding with diversity, awash in pluralism. The goal of social integration-once an American aim-has broken down as voices on all sides ignore the melting pot and argue instead for "ghettoization."

It would seem that Americans have forgotten that liberty depends on a widely shared conception of the desirable society. Without this conception, how can we evaluate the good or the deviant, our heroes and villains, the meritorious or the meretricious, ground our laws and resolve our conflicts?

In fact, it is no longer possible to distinguish between fame and infamy. Reality TV offers villains as heroes, thugs as role models. This is a culture that values diversity with a vengeance; one night call it "kaleidoscopic culture" because it changes daily in an effort to accommodate a newly defined subgroup.

There was a time when the public schools cultivated a sense of shared purpose; however, that purpose has succumbed to the pressure of diversity. Civil libertarians actively oppose any effort to encourage moral beliefs, contending that only relativism based on personal choice is constitutional.

As a consequence, students are often adrift in a sea of competing values, none with preferential tags attached to them. One might well ask how this nation can survive without a vital center. Of course, this does not mean that ethnic distinctiveness should be lost, nor does it mean that government should impose its version of virtue on the populace.

It does mean that voluntary efforts to construct a consensus of national principles should be enjoined. There is an American creed based on the Declaration of Independence, the Constitution, and the Federalist Papers that serve as a starting point in this effort at national integration. In addition, there are property rights, a rule of law, individual rights, a belief in liberty as a distinctive American value, the recognition of spiritual values, natural law, and a respect for the sanctity of life.

Societies can disintegrate or, at the very least, lose their character with unclear, shifting values. That is the danger we face at the moment. We seem to be suffering from moral anarchy as individual preference trumps any general principle. Even the word *doctrine* has been converted into a form of totalitarian compulsion.

What are the public forums for the display of virtue? Legalisms have replaced moral judgment; litigious exchanges have become a substitute for discussion and debate. The nation presumably negates a national identity through the superordination of pluralism.

Will this trend destroy the nation? It could if we do not direct our energies to unite disparate groups. Liberty does not depend on unanimity, but it does depend on unity. A disunited nation believing only in diversity could destroy what America values. This is not only a challenge facing future generations. It is the challenge for our time.

Notwithstanding the claim that all Americans share a common culture, there is fundamental discord in the land. It was evident when the newspapers of record argued that President Bush's success in the 2004 election was due primarily to the outpouring of support from the Evangelical community. The belief that religion should be relegated to a private concern-that it hasn't a place in the public square-is unstated but nonetheless intended.

It is worth asking, however, if the great majority of Americans want religion excluded from every aspect of public life. Despite the secular sentiments of many elites in America, most Americans profess a belief in God and few are inclined to deny the custom of giving thanks to God. Nevertheless, there is a powerful campaign underway to suppress religious expression.

Of course, individual believers can pray and sing hymns as long as these practices are done in private, away from giving offense to nonbelievers. This was a nation, however, founded by religious men that involved deep-seated conviction about the nexus between religion and the republic. Our currency doesn't say, "In mankind we trust," but rather, "In God we trust." The Constitution is an Augustinian document predicated on countervailing forces that are intended to restrain Original Sin.

Jean Jacques Rousseau[6], a philosopher whose views helped to inspire the French Revolution, wrote that liberty represents the abolition of all dependencies, such as the family and religion. As the founding fathers of this nation fully understood, however, without such alliances, without the mediating structures of family and church, the Social Contract cannot exist.

It is this Rousseauian vision, however, that haunts contemporary America. The lineaments of social organization are being challenged in every quarter. Respondents of gay marriage push an agenda that will cut the bonds of family ties. Secularists oppose the use of the expression, "One nation under God," in the Pledge of Allegiance. Avatars of late-term abortion are willing to engage in infanticide in order to maintain personal freedom.

Social order based on humility in the face of God has been reduced to basic materialism. I can recall the words of O'Brien in *1984*[7] who explains: "You are imagining that there is something called human nature which will be outraged by what we do and will turn against us. But we create human nature. Men are infinitely malleable." Alas, governments unrestrained by religious belief invariably try to mold human nature. Even though humans are malleable, they are certainly not infinitely malleable. Whether one accepts it or not there appears to be intelligent design in human nature.

Einstein noted that the earth was not organized with a simple throw of the dice, a chance moment in creation. Religion reaches for a vision of human nature beyond the material. It is most significant that it also is the antidote to solipsism and to a morality of "me." In the late 1960s Abbie Hoffman wrote *Do It!* If it feels good, do whatever it might be; however, feeling good and doing good are not the same. A society based on a personal sense of satisfaction cannot sustain itself.

A culture that likewise accepts anything that produces wealth will ultimately destroy itself as well. Wilhelm Roepke[8], a leading free-market economist, wrote, "the market does not create values, but consumes them and it must be constantly reimpregnated against rot."

The choice before Americans is the advancement of incremental rot or reimpregnation. One can use the value of materialism or the values that spring from religion. Adam Smith, author of the *Wealth of Nations* and sometimes described as the father of the free market, was also a moral philosopher. He recognized that a free-market unrestrained by virtue is ultimately corrosive.

From what roots does virtue spring? The answer is apparent to those who know the story of the nation's founding. It is also apparent in the order of the universe and intelligent design. As Browning noted, "God is in his heaven and all is right with the world." Well, all may not be right, but if God is not in his heaven, all would certainly be wrong.

Thomas Jefferson on behalf of the Founding Fathers of the United States noted in the First Amendment-and therefore a thought that was first in his thinking-that the government should not prohibit the free exercise of religion and it should not establish a national church or a sanctioned religious faith.

That said, it should be noted that Jefferson-a deist-pointed out that our national truths are derived from a Supreme Being and, as notably, the Constitution in conception is an Augustinian statement predicated on a belief in Original Sin.

Although the wall between church and state has grown higher in the last fifty years, it is probably fair to say that the founders had intentions different from the present reality.

The secularization of religion has been promoted through the "establishment clause," but an established religion is not the same as some form of religion. A crèche in a public square is not deemed a violation of the First Amendment, yet public prayer has been deemed a violation.

Tocqueville noted that religion in America is at the core of American life offering the moral precepts that give a culture texture. It is instructive that Richard Neuhaus, in *Naked Public Square*[9], makes the point that the public square is "naked" because religion as a public exercise has been eviscerated from contemporary life.

The debate continues. A pending Supreme Court decision on the use of publicly funded school vouchers for use in religious schools may have a lasting effect on the First Amendment's interpretation.

Americans, it is sometimes argued, are an increasingly religious people, albeit the nature of that religious observance is vague. The adamantine resistance by the ACLU and other church-state separatists to any public encroachment of religion, however, is not vague. It is a private matter, note these acolytes.

People freely and publicly identify themselves in myriad ways. Race is one form of identification, as is gender, and even sexual preference, but religion remains buried in privacy. One rarely hears anyone say publicly,

"I am a Catholic, Protestant, Jew, or Muslim." That is beyond normative claims.

In contending that the mere public expression of faith in God violates the establishment clause, atheists dictate public policy, and, as significantly, remove from the public square a traditional adherence to God.

As the search for meaning, even the search for sentience, continues in a world increasingly technocratic, spiritual demands are likely to increase. Where does that leave the secularized public square? My answer: On the road to desecularization.

The reforms of the last fifty years will not hold. America is likely to return to its roots in an outpouring of religious sentiment-what some have called "the Fourth Awakening."

I also suspect that Americans will return to the inspired vision of the Founders, who recognized the centrality of religion in the national culture, even as the establishment clause is honored.

This will not be an easy transition because the turn from the logical positivism of the recent past to spiritual inclinations is fraught with many possibilities, including irrationality. That is something to guard against.

Americans must remain open to revitalization of a culture bereft of morality and searching for guidance. Everyone benefits from that guidance, especially when the culture can dig its way out of the morass of depravity and into the bright light of vitality.

Chapter 2
The Age of Experimentation

Having lost respect for the values of our past, we lose the foundation of knowledge and wisdom on which good judgment depends.

When the American history of the late twentieth century is written with the benefit of sufficient hindsight, this will be called the era of experimentation. Ideas from the sublime, such as the discovery of DNA, to the ridiculous such, as Esalen, will be plumbed in an effort to make sense of this period.

Although it is probably premature to attach a label to the beginning of a new century, there is a condition coming into focus, a condition predicated on the rejection of absurd experimentation. In its most elemental form I would describe this current state as "Back to Basics" or BTB. It is already evident from relatively trifling issues like dieting to American foreign policy. Perhaps specifics would be helpful.

For decades Americans were told eating was fun and losing weight easy. An industry was created around weight loss fads. There was the ice cream diet, the water diet, the Atkins diet, the magic diet pills, Weight Watchers, and a host of others. It is now clear and indisputable, that if you use more calories than you consume, weight will be lost. This isn't hocus pocus, but basic arithmetic. Should someone consume 2500 calories a day, but maintain an activity level of 2000 calories, the waist and hips will expand.

If there is one area of life where experiments were on continual trial, it is education. From the open classroom to whole language study to the new math, educators displayed extraordinary imagination in organizing dubious programs. Students were told memorization is wrong; process is more important than outcomes; specifics in history such as dates are unnecessary, and all subjects are a reflection of power politics in one form or another.

After years of educational nonsense adopted as the next best experiment, President Bush and his Secretary of Education Paige argued for a return to drills, phonics, and "old-fashioned" methods of pedagogy. To the astonishment of many, even the teachers' unions seem to embrace this emerging standard, perhaps due-in no small part-to the obvious failure of the experiments they once adopted.

American business has seemingly come to its senses as well. In the high octane economy of the late 1990s it was easy to believe that PE ratios don't count and that the laws of financial transactions had been repealed by new economic development.

Now that the bubble has burst and it is increasingly evident valuations in the 1990s were often fictional, fundamentals have regained appeal. Value rather than growth is suddenly in vogue. Moreover, earnings-once dismissed by a Wall Street guru as telling you nothing important about a company-now tell a great deal.

Even psychology, that great warren of ridiculous ideas, is reevaluating its past and recommending the logical and, I might add obvious, recommendations on everything from child development to courtship. The 1960s recipe for self-actualization led to one accident after another on the rocky shoals of freedom without limits. There is a price to pay for instant gratification that cannot be overlooked. "If it feels good do it" died with a generation of strung out drug addicts.

Moreover, the contention that if you have it, flaunt it is wrong as well. Show-offs are usually knocked off their pedestal. Walk humbly in the face of God is reemerging as a welcome code of deportment, even though Hollywood hasn't yet imbibed that message.

Has the nation come to its senses based on my examples? Have the extreme experiments of the last half of the twentieth century been interred? In my judgment the true believers of hoaxes and fantasies will not disappear. A sucker is born every minute, and it's often impossible to dispel silly ideas even with rational argument and incontrovertible evidence. Nonetheless, there are hopeful signs. BTB appears to be catching on. As soon as buttons appear with BTB letters and red, white, and blue ribbons are worn on one's lapel, the counterrevolution will be in full swing. Who knows, perhaps the new century will be the age of restoration. It happened after Napoleon; maybe now it will happen after Dr. Spock.

The "Leave It To Beaver" mom, the prototypical television parent in the 1960s was a loyal spouse who could always be found at 3:30 pm serving milk and cookies to her kids who came home from school.

On television, however, these wholesome women have been transformed into "Desperate Housewives," women who are narcissistic, adulterous, and generally oblivious to their children.

Although television programming invariably reaches for the extreme, there is something revealing about the changed national cultural conditions in these two examples.

At the risk of hyperbole, it would appear that America is in the throes of a cultural revolution whose emphasis is on the abandonment of traditions. Such words as *modesty, rectitude,* and *discipline* have been replaced by *freedom, self-indulgence,* and *license.* Even taboos now have their rationalizers.

In the novel *Kiss*[1] the author tries to justify incest. Many rap artists (I use the word loosely) such as Snoop Dogg are intent on combining music and pornographic videos. In such widely heralded films such as *American Beauty* adult-teenage sexual relationships are depicted graphically. Even at the Super Bowl-perhaps the major family event of the year-Janet Jackson revealed her breast during a "clothing mishap,"-"wardrobe malfunction" a condition Frank Rich at the *New York Times* reflexively defended. The cultural air is replete with examples.

In fact, as William Buckley noted, pornography is ubiquitous. It is found on billboards, on the sides of buses, in clothing brochures, and in television ads. One car company ad intentionally relied on "key exchanges" with ambiguous lascivious glaring in order to promote its SUV.

This, of course, is only one dimension of the coarsening of culture. As a New York subway rider raised in an antediluvian era, I still give up my seat to an elder person. If I don't guard that seat till the very last second, however, a teenager will pounce on it. On several occasions, I've asked the adolescent to give the seat up only to hear a burst of four letter expletives.

There is scarcely a rap song that doesn't encourage the abuse of women. Some even suggest that a broom handle be inserted in every female orifice. Women are regarded as prostitutes; there for the bemusement and delectation of predatory males.

The question that might be asked is how can traditions possibly be restored in this cultural wasteland. There is admittedly a Gresham's Law of culture in which the bad drives the good out of circulation. Nonetheless, there are opportunities for restoration when one considers the many media outlets that now exist.

Efforts should be made to create beachheads of civility in schools and in places of worship that ban cursing and demand courteous behavior. Despite some reservations I have about the conversion of books into films, the manner and courtship practices in the Jane Austen novels converted into movies could serve as models of appropriate behavior.

The Blackstone catalogue has scores of audio books that can easily be converted into popular fare. Ian McClellan's *Iliad* is simply a breathtaking example of a classic tale made accessible and inviting.

Teachers who have been trained in a system of pedagogical relativism should be made to realize that existentialism is utterly at odds with laws and norms. In society-as Aristotle noted-we are all political animals seeking refuge and solace in a community of shared values.

Instead of offering what may be uplifting, the modern museum, with rare exception, provides a menu of the shocking, degrading, and politically incorrect, and its myrmidons defend its shows as manifestations of "anti-art" or as a critique of bourgeois sensibility; however, there are opportunities to initiate shows of artistic spirit and aesthetic brilliance in the hundreds of museums that exist in communities hungry for culture.

What can be done-in my judgment-is somewhere between retreat and resistance. I call it the "oasis strategy." In some respects the oasis strategy recreates the approach of Antonio Gramsci, whose radical minions marched through the cultural institutions until their numbers represented a critical mass.

Whenever there are openings, traditionalists should try to do the same thing (i.e., to advance their agenda by "leavening" institutions now dominated by radicals). There are many edifying cultural institutions that exist, but they must be cultivated and cherished as the response to cultural degradation.

Franz Kafka[2] once wrote, "There is always hope, but not for us." It is a clever line, but untrue. Hope exists in the cultivation of our own little gardens, rejecting the demeaning and restoring the uplifting. It won't be easy, but it is better than caving in to the crudities of a culture in decay.

I recently overheard a conversation in which a young man said to his friend, "Listen to your feelings." Of course, even if you listen, there isn't much you will hear.

There is a growing belief, that we must break the chains of rational thought and find the liberating light of our feelings. Notice how often people say "I feel..." instead of "I think..." Notice as well that feelings are worn as a hirsute, an attachment to sensibility. "I feel, therefore I am," apologies to Descartes.

Even more extreme than the emphasis on feelings is forbidden feelings. The fascination with Hannibal Lecter, Dungeons and Dragons, and the philosophy of Friedrich Nietzsche are the classic illustrations of this sentiment. For avatars of this form of feeling crossing normative boundaries is inevitable, a journey to the islands of perversity.

Then there is irresistible feeling, an inexorable impulse that one can do no other than what is done. This is presumably a class of feelings built into one's genetic disposition: "My genes made me do it," a variant on the extra Y chromosome theory as an explanation for criminal behavior.

The utilitarians have their own version of feelings summarized by, "If it feels good, do it." Alas, many have adopted a world view that subordinates morality to pleasurable feelings, even when seeking pleasure may cause others pain or promote social chaos.

No one can deny the existence of "higher" feelings, an aesthetic of enjoying the good, the true and the beautiful because they are examples of the best the human imagination can conjure. A cousin of higher feeling is spiritual sentiment, the reaching for the transcendent.

Keats[3] gave form to these feelings in his words, "I am certain of nothing but of the holiness of the heart's affections and the truth of imagination... I have the same idea of all our passions as of love: they are all, in their sublime, creative of essential beauty."

Although feelings can be treacly and saccharine, especially when overdone, they are not unimportant. They give texture to our lives. Moreover, they offer harmony if used in conjunction with rationality. The problem is that in isolation they are not self-interpreting; rather, they are certainly not the master of rational exegesis.

Feelings are unquestionably part of the human design. But they often go beyond design; rather than see them as part of the big picture of life, they sometimes become the big picture. The moral manifestation of feelings, for example, often rejects morality, just as feelings often oppose empirical evidence and even common sense.

How often does the teenager listen to his feelings rather than his parents? Why does the revolutionary rely on his feelings rather than understanding? Rebellion, as the clearest expression of feelings, has an intoxicating appeal. The rebel listens *only* to his or her feelings.

One would hope that insinuating itself into the panoply of feelings is virtue, a belief that there are borders that should not be crossed. This hope, of course, is challenged each day by the believers in forbidden feelings. The snipers who killed Virginia and Maryland residents, did so because of dark, morose, misguided, and ultimately evil feelings. They were men without virtue.

It is instructive that feelings, framed by reason and ordained by the understanding of the common good, can address the concerns of the free individual and a sense of societal liberty. Feelings can set us free or imprison; they are the cause of our frustration and the call to a higher purpose.

Obi-Wan Kenobi says, "Luke, trust your feelings!" But it is not clear if he should trust those feelings. Fortunately, he follows his heart rather than his mind and the "Evil Empire" in the *Star Wars* film is defeated. Is a morality of feeling, all on which we should rely? It is far better to challenge the heart with the mind in a test of wills. Feelings will be all the better for it, albeit feelings should not be confused with sentimentality.

If there is one condition that afflicts America at the moment it is fake sentimentality, a false emotion that manifests itself whenever a negative news story appears.

Take the events at Virginia Tech, for example. At every one of the candle light vigils in which violence was decried, spokesmen referred to the "tragedy" of 32 murdered victims. The tragedy that eluded the hand-wringing wasn't a tragedy at all. A tragedy is related to an inevitable event (e.g. those who are in a hurricane or a tornado).

The murders at Virginia Tech could have been prevented had the administration at the university, the courts, and everyone else who had contact with Mr. Cho acted appropriately. It wasn't a tragedy; it was simply bloody, gruesome murder. All of the lamentations about guns and violence won't change a thing because they do not deal with the essence of the crime. Of course, the lamentation isn't designed to deal with the crime, but rather to make observers feel better about themselves, a self-righteous display of good intentions.

The reaction to Imus' stupid comment about "nappy headed ho's" on the Rutgers women's basketball team was similarly patently false. It strains credulity to believe the women on this team never heard a rap "artist" use this language. When the team appeared on Oprah, players expressed their shock (!) that such language could be leveled against them. I am certainly not defending Imus' rant, but it is hard to believe the women on this team could be so offended by the use of the word "ho" when it is commonly employed by rappers all the time and, as notable, can be heard on the streets of every urban ghetto in the nation.

Then there is the new "hip" embrace of a limited carbon footprint or what some call the carbon diet. Celebrities now rush to embrace the environmental friendly agenda of Al Gore among others. A carbon-cutting business has sprung up overnight that discusses-in minute detail-emissions. Of course, the proponents of this position ignore what is going on in India and China, the two most populous nations on the globe. Nor do they consider the actual result of the carbon-setting campaign in the United States.

In actuality, if carbon cutting does anything, it makes its proponents feel good. After all, they are doing something to save us from ourselves-or so they think. As Andrew Revkin writing in the *New York Times* (4/29/07) noted, "The carbon-neutral campaign is a sign of the times-easy on the sacrifice and big on the consumerism."

Despite this campaign, it is unlikely that greenhouse gases will decrease. Nor is the science on this matter as incontrovertible as Al Gore suggests. If one realizes that the campaign is less about an environmental effect then the psychological affirmation signing on gives its adherents, it makes eminent sense.

Faux reactions, of course, aren't new. The nation is often caught up in them as the Alar scare and the hysteria over DDT would indicate; however, I would contend the nation is reaching for new extremes, new levels of fake sentimentality.

In the end, whatever the full efflorescence of this phenomenon may be, it will be hard to get an appropriate (read: realistic) response to any condition. Will political correctness-now observed as a national creed-trump self-preservation? Will handwringing serve as a purging ritual for the nation rather than action?

As I see it, fake sentiment isn't benign. It beguiles its intended audience into a sense that something has been accomplished. It has that feel good dimension to it which in the end is about as satisfying as chewing gum on an empty stomach.

Years ago some educators introduced the "self-esteem campaign" for students that suggested that if only students would feel good about themselves academic performance would improve. Needless to say, that didn't happen. Needless to say as well, all of the fake sentiment that surrounds current cultural movements won't improve our lot in life either.

There was a time when parents were principally concerned with the physical well-being of their children. When kids left the house, parents would say "be well." That was decades ago.

In this increasingly psychologized era personal happiness is the goal. Parents invariably ask "are you happy?" In fact, happiness has been transmogrified from a wish into a right.

The Declaration of Independence enshrined "the pursuit of happiness" as a right, even though Jefferson probably meant to suggest a pursuit constrained by standards of virtue and respect, and not mere psychological satisfaction.

At the moment the entire culture manufactures happiness industries. Unhappiness has been medicalized as a form of depression requiring Prozac or its equivalent. Aging has been addressed by the obsession with plastic surgery. Physical beauty is so sought after that cosmetics firms promise it and magazines tell you how to find it.

Young people grow up with the illusion physical beauty can be bought and that happiness supersedes the requirements of civic responsibility.

Bertrand Russell[4] once wrote about the dangers of "self-centered passions" arguing that people should be encouraged to acquire "those affections and interests which will prevent our thoughts dwelling perpetually on ourselves."

It is curious that the entire culture promotes self-centered passions. From the publication of "I'm Okay; You're Okay[5]" to the present *Oprah* magazine, vanity of celebrities and lesser lights is on display.

There is the constant droning from Hollywood personalities about how life has treated them unfairly and how they suffer. Alas, in some cases that is probably true, but it's hard to identify with the suffering starlet who receives $20 million a film.

These celebrities want happiness-or so they say-the aspiration that knows no limits. What is wrong with a dose of unhappiness?

Were it not for unhappiness Napoleon would not have overcome the chiding of his schoolmates to become Emperor of France. Were it not for unhappiness Lincoln would not have found the vision to keep the Union intact. Were it not for unhappiness Teddy Roosevelt could not have overcome boyhood infirmities to reach the heights of political success.

Unhappiness certainly does not lead inexorably to greatness, but in many cases it does inspire greatness. Moreover, happiness is neither inevitable nor made to last. There are mood swings in life that everyone experiences; the happiness of today may be the melancholy of tomorrow.

Perhaps that explains why La Rochefoucauld[6] said, "One is never as happy or as unhappy as one thinks." The word *happiness* represents a presumptive bliss, an ecstasy that transcends the limits of biology. Americans are being told to pursue this chimera with all the energy they can muster and all the money they can spend.

For many, an abstraction has been converted into material things as commodities are invested with spiritual power. A new car will make you sexy. A new television set will offer insight about world affairs. A cruise will let the "real you" emerge. In the end, things will make you happy.

Drifting in a sea of existential feelings, with media proclamations calling for the search for happiness, the average person-indeed most people-doesn't know to which shore to turn to for refuge. He or she is in a quandary over how it can be reached, albeit the next purchase may be the bridge to the Promised Land.

"A lifetime of happiness!" declared George Bernard Shaw[7], "It should be hell on earth." That discovery has not yet been made as contemporary utopians desperately pursue happiness at any price.

That pursuit has run into many potholes. If there is fragmentation in America, and alas this condition is undeniable, it is related to a divorce rate 30 percent higher than 1970, a marriage rate that has dropped 40 percent since 1970, and an illegitimacy rate that has skyrocketed from 5 percent in 1960 to 33 percent today.

The number of couples repudiating marriage in favor of nonmarital cohabitation is as dramatic. In the last two decades this nonmarital status number has increased three times. The number of female-headed households with children has similarly risen from 3 million in 1970 to 8 million today.

During the same three decade period (1970 to 2000) married couples with children declined from 25.5 million to 25 million despite a 30 percent increase in the total population. Among children who live with married parents, only a little over half live with both biological parents; the rest reside with a remarried biological parent or a step parent.

No matter where one stands politically, the retreat from marriage and traditional family life cannot be treated as some innocuous shift in lifestyle. This condition is having a profound effect on American life even though the effects are infrequently discussed.

From a Tocqevillian standpoint the family was one of those meditating institutions essential in transmitting cultural traditions and the habits of mind that result in good citizenship. If America is disunited it is due in no small part to the breakdown in marriage and the surrogate parents tending to children when mom is in the workplace.

Rather than serve as a center for repose and contentment, the family has emerged as a battleground where divorced parents fight over childcare payments and visitation rights. *Leave It To Beaver* has been converted into *War of The Roses*.

The internal family battles unfortunately often have a disintegrating influence on the nation. For example, males born to unmarried mothers were 1.7 times more likely to be a criminal offenders and 2.1 times more likely to become a chronic offender than males born to married mothers. It is instructive that 87 percent of those incarcerated in American prisons either don't know who their father is or have not had any contact with fathers in years.

It is curious that as the family institution is threatened, gender politics has become more extreme. Many radical feminists contend marriage is unnecessary and left-wing social critics define the family in increasingly latitudinarian ways. It is not surprising that divorced women tend to be more inclined to accept radical feminist views than married counterparts, a clear line in the political sand.

The retreat from family life also has its manifestation in economic life. Family disintegration is the gorge between rich and poor with rich people more likely to emerge from stable families and poor people tending to be the products of female-headed families. The so-called haves and have-nots are less a function of wealth than family life.

Family decay is unquestionably the number one social problem in America, yet many deny that reality arguing that newly won rights give women freedom they never had before and society should not move backwards. Moreover, children do not have a political voice. The self-fulfillment sought by mom or dad might have a deleterious effect on their kids. In an age of immediate gratification the children are often lost in the calculus.

In the present *zeitgeist* even healthy, stable families are affected by the social detritus around them. It is not as if family disunity can be contained. Illegitimacy makes the schools less effective and the streets less safe. The freedom for easy divorce often leads to the rupture of friendship and neighborhood cohesion. The specter of family disunity encourages an unwillingness to commit and a fear of marriage and children.

Family disunity is the microcosm of national disunity. As families face unraveling, so, too, do the bonds that hold America together. If we are to restore one nation indivisible, united by common threads, then we need families intact, stable, and united as well. We have gone down a path of licentious self-absorption for decades and have paid the price with societal flotsam and jetsam. The time has come to restore the family as the center of American life and recognize its value in keeping us together.

We might also recognize the price of disunity-namely dysfunctional social behavior-that undermines the nation's health.

At a recent briefing by John Walters-the nation's drug czar-drug use patterns by youthful offenders were outlined. After falling steeply between 1979 and 1991, the favorable trend reversed as drug abuse climbed steeply between 1992 and 1997, when it reached a plateau. Starting in 2001 a favorable trend downward was reestablished, resulting in an aggregate 19 percent decline by 2006.

Although it is easy to overemphasize short-term statistical information, it is also true that young people who are initiated to drug use in their teen years are at far greater risk for dependency than those who begin drug use during maturation. Even more compelling, young people who do not use drugs by age 18 to 20 are highly unlikely to ever develop drug dependency. Hence, driving down drug use during this youthful period is critical in the overall assessment of this national trend.

That said, albeit unmentioned by John Walters, the pattern of drug use is seemingly correlated to the party leader occupying the White House. For example, youthful drug use rose from 1977 to 1981, while Carter was president, declined from 1981 to 1991 when Reagan and Bush I were presidents, rose from 1992 to 2001 when Clinton was president, and had been in a steady decline from 2001 under Bush II. Is there a relationship between the party in power and the rise and fall of drug use? Are the statistics mere anomalies? Is there a view about drugs implicitly or explicitly communicated by Democrats and Republicans that results in the rise and fall of drug abuse?

Causal relationships and correlations obviously enter the realm of speculation. Nonetheless, the evidence is suggestive. Could it be that Carter and Clinton, the two Democratic presidents in this thirty-year history, were inclined to deemphasize resistance to youthful drug use or did they communicate implicit messages that condoned such use? Clinton did admit to marijuana use, even though he didn't inhale. Bush II readily admits to alcohol abuse, albeit he is an avid teetotaler who warns against the dangers of alcoholism. My suspicion is this may be extreme speculation leading to unwarranted conclusions.

It might be a more fruitful line of inquiry to see the cultural tone set by the respective parties. If Hollywood is any guide-clearly a dubious guide-Republican leaders are invariably portrayed as uptight, narrow-minded, and frigid. In one segment of the aformentioned *Desperate Housewives*, a leading character finds herself in bed about to engage in sexual activity, when she looks up at her lover and says, "I can't do it; I'm a Republican." This is presumably a laugh line.

There may, however curious, be an element of truth to this situation. Is it possible that Republicans, who tend to be more traditional and religious than their Democratic counterparts, are also more concerned about normative moral principles? This judgment obviously may vary within parties as well. There was a difference between Senators Kennedy and Lieberman. Moreover, when the moral card is employed it applies to Republican Congressman Foley as well as Democratic Congressman Franks. Nuance is clearly critical. It should also be noted as Tom Wolfe once argued that "moralisms are the foxholes for incompetents." Surely one should be careful in casting about moral arguments.

When one considers the charges leveled against President Bush, it seems reasonable that he should take credit for a reduction in youthful drug use, despite my already mentioned hesitation. After all, he's been charged with neglect after Hurricane Katrina, mistreatment of captured terrorists, and a host of other malefactions he probably had no way of controlling. Because presidents get blamed for everything that goes wrong, they should get some credit for things that go right.

Moreover, it may be that Republican presidents set a tone and forceful strictures that influence drug policy. The evidence is not dispositive, but it is suggestive, and in the present Washington environment that isn't bad.

Leaving partisanship aside, it seems that we are moving to a period of increasing paternalism. *The Chronicle of Higher Education* (May 9, 2008) devoted four full pages to a new book by two professors at the University of Chicago, Richard Thaler and Cass Sunshine, one a professor of economics and behavioral science and the other a professor of law. The book, entitled *Nudge: Improving Decisions About Health, Wealth and Happiness*[12], is intended to approach policies that encourage, but do not insist on, socially desirable directions.

Cognitive limitations presumably stand in the way of appropriate choices. Because people are basically inert, impulsive, and often irrational they would be best off nudged into acceptable behavior, claim the authors. They call for "libertarian paternalism," which they argue is not an oxymoron.

A "nudge," according to them, is a noncoercive alteration in the decision-making process (e.g., innocuous details such as the pattern of lines on a road). Professor Sunshine explains, "For too long, the United States has been trapped in a debate between laissez-faire types who believe markets will solve all our problems and the command and control types who believe that if there is a market failure then you need a mandate." He and his colleague stand astride arguing that an understanding of human irrationality can improve how public and private institutions shape policy. The presumption is that a nudge does not limit free choice; it merely provides a desirable direction.

One example used by the authors is the reluctance of employees to sign up for 401k plans even though it is in their best interest to do so. They suggest that companies adopt automatic enrollment, while retaining an opt-out provision. That would be seen as the right kind of nudge that still allows for free choice.

Professor Thaler has spent a career thinking about decision making. In his judgment, people often opt for irrational or overly optimistic positions. For example, he notes they are more fearful of unlikely threats like a nuclear power accident than they are something more probable like a car accident.

As I see it this book is yet another academic argument for the "third way," a path between the free market and the command economy that has failed so many times before. The problem is that the "nudge" will come from the same government and the same bureaucrats often responsible for failures in the public sector. It is surely fair to say that people sometimes make irrational and undesirable choices in life, but isn't that often true of bureaucrats who have the same temptations? Are Thaler and Sunshine merely indicating that there are intelligent social engineers who can tell us how to behave?

It seems to me that if you are paternalistic in subliminally nudging someone in the "right direction" you cannot be a libertarian, even if the nudge is intended to be noncoercive. Moreover, even when there are rewards for certain behavior that are well established and well understood, some people choose to ignore them. For example, there is an unquestionable correlation between education and a standard of living. A college degree is worth more than a high school diploma and a PhD is worth more than a college degree. Is there anyone who doesn't know this? Many still cannot be nudged into higher education.

As noted, Professor Thaler argues that many people are more fearful of unlikely threats than probable threats. Thaler must surely realize that threats are related to perceptions. As a result of the *China Syndrome* there is the fear that a nuclear explosion could have widespread and catastrophic consequences, however limited the probability. A traffic accident-even though more probable-has limited consequences and is something already integrated into one's consciousness.

The market mechanism clearly isn't perfect, but it does account for irrational choices and it assumes as well the ultimate prevalence of what the public wants. I would prefer the "invisible hand" to the manipulated hand of social engineers. How long would it take for the subtle nudge to become, as the estimable Roger Kimball put it, the big push? Is it enough to say, as Thaler and Sunshine do, that transparency is sufficient to offset the nudging of social engineers? After all, a free economy works because of its freedom, which includes the freedom to know. As the authors note people still make irrational decisions.

It is an illusion to think that there are appropriate alternatives to the free market despite the clever conflation of words in the Thaler-Sunshine thesis. In the end, of course, paternalism is not liberty and liberty cannot be paternalism.

Hubris, the sin of overweening pride or arrogance, is similarly invariably the condition that undermines societies and individuals in classical literature. We forgot that hubris has its influence on contemporary society as well.

Thus, we return to: "If you've got it, flaunt it," the modern expression of hubristic sentiment. In a recent *Money Central* article, it is noted that John Chambers, chairman of Cisco, predicted a continued 30-50 percent annual growth in his company. One year after the prediction, the company had three straight quarters of 70 percent profit declines. There appears to be a price to be paid for boasting.

Kenneth Lay, former CEO of Enron, characterized his company as a New Economy firm "before it became cool to be one." On August 14, 2001, he sent an e-mail to employees noting, "Our performance has never been stronger, our business model has never been more robust. We have the finest organization in American business today." Now, of course, the company is in ruins, employees are out of work, pensions have been converted to dust and criminal proceedings may await the principals.

Whereas Joe Namath did predict a victory for the New York Jets in the 1969 Super Bowl that proved to be correct, sports aficionados are usually disappointed by assertions of victory. Patrick Ewing, formerly with the New York Knicks, predicted victory for his team during every playoff series in which he was involved, but he was never correct.

The *Wall Street Journal*[15] noted that of companies that bought the rights to name stadiums after themselves often fell into bankruptcy or financial difficulty. Examples include Enron, T.W.A., PSI Net, Fruit of the Loom, 3 Com, Conseco, and CMGI Inc.

Hubris usually leads to invincibility, and a belief in invincibility leads to complacency and failure. In *The Speculator*, written by Victor Niederhoffer and Laurel Kenner[10], a real estate attorney is quoted who points out that companies putting up huge edifices to celebrate their success soon find company fortunes declining. This obviously isn't true for all companies, but such examples as the GM building in midtown Manhattan, the IBM tower, the AT&T edifice, and the E.F. Hutton building are interesting cases that enhance the claim.

46 The Transformational Decade

Another dimension of hubris is gratuitous celebration. Joe Paterno, the coach at Penn State, maintains that if one of his players scores a touchdown, celebration isn't warranted. He notes, "You don't want opponents to think it's the first time you've been in the end zone." The Paterno view is a rarity. Now almost all players dance and jive. In the XFL football league players were encouraged to do so. Perhaps it is not coincidental that the league is no longer in existence.

After the vice-president at Delta Airlines said, "We are the best in the business," the stock price declined by 31 percent.

Those companies claiming to be the best or athletes acting as if they are the best are, in many instances, poised for a fall. To some degree this downside of self-congratulation applies to nations as well.

When economic prophets argued in the 1980s that Japan's form of a command economy had solved the riddles of the free market's roller coaster effect, many investors and some Japanese leaders believed the press clippings. At the time, the Nikkei Index was in the neighborhood of 35,000. Today when fifty percent of the value in the market has been lost, both analysts and Japanese leaders are singing a different tune

If there is a lesson to be learned, it is good things happen to those who have it and don't flaunt it. I wouldn't invest long on Donald Trump's success since his financial empire has been constructed on hubristic impulses. Even Martha Stewart[11] once argued, "I can bend steel with my mind. I can bend anything if I try hard enough." Ms. Stewart clearly learned that the gods do not reward those who are egotistical enough to believe they can reshape the world.

Keep in mind hubris should not be confused with confidence. Faith in oneself is healthy and possibly rewarding; it is arrogance and pride that do in successful people, institutions, and nations.

My notion of success is by no means foolproof, but I would bet on the team that does the least showboating and is disinclined to guarantee victory. After all, the gods will be watching.

Indeed, confidence has been one critical dimension of our national history. In his 1964 commencement address at the University of Michigan, President Lyndon Johnson argued that most of American history had been devoted to "subduing the continent," and the result of American "unbounded invention and untiring industry" had been "an order of plenty for our people." As a consequence, he noted, our new goal would be to discover and employ the "wisdom...to enrich and elevate our national life and to advance the quality of American civilization." Here were the essential elements of the Great Society programs: abundance beyond scarcity and liberty beyond conventional limitations.

Once these goals were achieved, a new nation would presumably be created "where leisure is a welcome place to build and reflect, and not a feared cause of boredom and restlessness," as well as one "where the city of man serves not only the needs of the body and the demands of commerce but the desire for beauty and the hunger for community."

In this speech are the undiluted positions of the M & M boys, Marx and Maslow: Marxism as the triumph over scarcity and the "inexorable" march to sharing the fruits of production, and Maslow and the search for personal fulfillment and the psychology of contentment.

This speech and these aspirations were delivered two decades before Francis Fukuyama's[12] famous *National Interest* article on the "End of History," yet in many ways it presaged the Fukuyama thesis. A new age was about to be born that transcends the so-called permanent features of human nature. Scarcity was to be relegated to the ash heap of history and unbounded liberty would produce the flourishing of culture.

History, however, has a curious way of insinuating itself into this idealistic equation. What is to be done if the "permanent features of human nature" cannot be transcended? Suppose scarcity reappears in the form of a financial breakdown. Suppose as well that liberty is challenged by a new, virulent form of totalitarianism that has an accompanying religious fervor.

The new millennium has reawakened a somnolent historical beast. A defeated Soviet Union has been restored as an active imperial power eager to regain the "near-abroad," those nations once within its orbit. Communism may be dead, but the lust for power is very much in the ascendancy.

China, once the sleeping giant of Asia, has awakened and is flexing its economic strength and military muscle in regional matters from the Taiwan Strait to the Sea of Japan.

Islam, flush with petrodollars and a belief that the West is in retreat, weakened by its debauched culture, is challenging for global hegemony. For radical Islamists the seventh century has returned along with dreams of caliphates from Madrid to Jakarta.

In addition, there is the collapse of American credit markets roiled by politicians who believe nirvana in the form of home ownership could be created on the basis uncollateralized mortgages. These pollyannas were joined by greedy Wall Street brokers who saw sugar plums in mortgage-backed securities underwritten on exotic dreams. With the collapse of the credit market came the inevitable reintroduction of historical reality for many Americans.

Scarcity has not disappeared. Moreover, for many, the unconstrained life has discovered constraints. All at once America has been forced to consider bourgeois virtues of sobriety, delayed gratification, hard work, and resourcefulness. Easy money is easily evaporated.

Visions of abundance have been challenged, and the self-indulgence associated with the generational pursuit of "finding oneself" is now a luxury many can no longer afford. Trust fund investments are starting to recede.

These conditions clearly may be temporary. History may also recede in time. I believe that the permanent conditions of human nature are indeed permanent. We may choose to ignore them because they are inconvenient or inconsistent with our dreams, but they have a way of reappearing.

It is wise to consider our collective hubris. Like Icarus we may soar for a time, but when we get too close to the sun our wings of wax melt and we will come crashing back to earth. History speaks with a certain inevitability always sensitive to human nature and instincts. In fact one can argue that lessons of history are immutable.

If the 9/11 commission hearings indicated anything at all, it is that the nation was divided over the war in Iraq. It often seemed as if partisan issues transcended national welfare. The danger we faced is that the political climate could lead to stasis or a retreat in the war on terrorism.

Whether Americans will resign themselves to an attenuated war on terrorism and make the requisite sacrifice, as was done during the Cold War or will fasten onto a positive vision of the future will ultimately make all the difference in this conflict.

To suggest that the United States faces new, more fearsome dangers than was ever the case before is to state the obvious. Everyone realizes weapons of mass destruction and the manifold ways in which they can be delivered pose a threat qualitatively different from any in the past.

It remains to be seen whether a high-income, low-birthrate nation like the United States can tolerate the loss of American soldiers daily in

Iraqi. It is already clear that some members of the press corps have adopted the Ted Kennedy position that the war in Iraq is the twenty-first-century Vietnam quagmire.

As I see it, we must guard against fatalism, a fear that conditions are out of control and we have neither the will nor means to deal with them. Based on the hearings in Washington one might well be left with the impression that our counterintelligence efforts were feeble and bureaucratic infighting militated against the prophylactic devices the nation expects from its government.

Overcoming this growing fatalism and sustaining national *esprit*, despite the tocsin in the air, is a national imperative. How it can be done isn't easily determined.

Writing in the 1950s, the sociologist Pitirim Sorokin argued, "A fairly uniform symptom of disintegration in any culture is the substitution of quantitative colossalism for a sublime quality; of glittering externality for inner value; of a show for a substance."

The feverish tempo of accelerated change that is part and parcel of contemporary life surely tends to diminish adherence to lasting values.

Here, then, is the challenge for a people that have already faced so many dangers: to retain a vision of the nation that upholds its heritage and is capable of defending its present.

The United States holds the key to civilization. Should the nation's willingness to defend itself and its international interest falter, life will never be the same. Americans fight both for self-defense against sanguinic and shadowy foes and for the foundations of Western civilization in Scripture, literature, traditions, and morality.

Our test at the moment was a test of will. There is little doubt that the ordeal we faced-the bloodshed and the threats-have already led to catharsis, a national soul-searching that resulted in one shining moment after 9/11 in philosophical solidarity, if not political unity.

The eternal lessons of life and death are perpetually forgotten and then recalled. People must live through anguish in order to discover enlightenment. Life is alpha and omega, with the cosmic flow taking microcosmic forms. As a result, world history is a contest in which the strong, the determined and the self-assured triumph.

If true, this notion suggests that the United States cannot be defeated unless its determination wanes. A victory on the battlefield is sometimes preceded by a depletion of will. Hence, overcoming fatalism translates into the maintenance of superior military strength and support for the national characteristics that give determination vitality.

Because I don't have evidence to substantiate the claim I suspect that the seed of national piety-perhaps the reemergence of a civic religion would be a better way of putting it-is starting to emerge. It sprang from a tortured conscience, from the trials of the moment, from spiritual hunger, and from a search for meaning in a world made barren by the depredations in popular culture.

Those who believe that war is unnecessary or cannot solve any problem are now finding it difficult to turn the other cheek after 3000 of their fellow Americans were killed at the World Trade Center for no other reason except their American heritage. Accommodationists are baffled by an enemy that has only destruction as its goal. Many Americans wonder when the scourge of terrorism will abate and when our armies or God's grace will grant tranquility. They wait in vain, for our enemy is intent on testing our mettle, our essential national fortitude.

One condition necessary to sustain cultural vitality is a national tradition, a common understanding of the nation's founding and history so that the efforts of the past can animate the present. The transmission of tradition does not require a great leader or a single spokesman; rather, it does require history that reveals achievement as much as imperfection. Revisionists unfortunately so dominate the historical profession that mainly mistakes and misdeeds qualify for investigation. This is a tragedy whose effect is already evident in youngsters unfamiliar with the nation's past and in amnesia about history as a ubiquitous condition.

A recent report by the American Council of Trustees and Alumni[13], "The Hollow Core: Failure of the General Education Curriculum," indicates that most college students can graduate without having studied American history or American government.

The unity of America's disparate people is predicated on an idea, a collective consciousness and a common destiny. A sense of the past is a source of all future collective action. To instill this sense requires an exalted leap that goes beyond the personal and the present. It requires a vision of what ought to be. This vision, I should hastily note, is not one devoted to material conditions. History has demonstrated repeatedly that rich nations may produce indulges that can enervate the soul and sap the spirit. It is wise to recall that the external trappings of power have typically failed to save many empires from collapse, however impressive they may have seemed in their time.

The United States must guard against such indulgences and simultaneously instill a knowledge of respect for its past glory and unique accomplishments. This nation cannot allow itself to be deflated from without or weakened from within. Nations survive for many reasons, not the least of which is civic pride-a belief that the idea behind the nation is worth defending, and if events call for it, sacrificing one's life. Nations remain strong so long as their citizens can utter with pride the words, "I believe." These words serve as a bulwark against the understandable impulse to seek safety, insulation from the horrors on the world stage.

America as an inspired idea-notwithstanding her many detractors across the globe-is sufficient reason for overcoming fatalism; however, in the midst of mangled and burned bodies and blood on the streets of Fallujah and elsewhere, idealism seems a faraway impulse.

It is precisely in the moment of despair that reminders of the past should be evoked. The words "I believe" are the armor against the day's horrible headlines. They are words forged into the national psyche; however, they are also easily forgotten unless passed on from one generation to the next.

In the middle of the bloodiest battles of the Civil War President Abraham Lincoln was disconsolate. Seeking solace from despair, the president turned to his minister who suggested the words in the bible might be comforting. Lincoln proceeded to read the bible and there in the Book of Proverbs he found words that were indeed helpful in overcoming depression: "When there is no vision, a people perish."

Those words are as true now as they were then. They give comfort now as they did then. They also offer a challenge. We must seek to reclaim our vision as a nation and understand what we must defend and why we must do so now. To do any less is to lose all we value.

Chapter 3
The Slippery Slope of Cultural Degradation

Can the forces of culture be returned to normative standards or is cultural inertia impossible to turn around?

Pitirim Sorokin, the brilliant social thinker, argued that history is cyclical going through periods that are ideational, ideological, and sensate. Affluent societies, which can afford to indulge themselves, revert to pleasures that appeal to the senses as their overarching concern. Whereas sensate societies are dissolute, Sorokin contends that subordinate ideational ideas in sensate cultures will become superordinate, thereby replacing the sensual in an inexorable cycle. What if the society amuses itself to extinction? What if complacency militates against arousal? Suppose the sensate condition is so dominant recreation cannot take place?

That these questions are asked is due, in no small part, to the willingness of the public to accept many of the changes foisted on the nation by the Obama administration. It strikes me as remarkable that a government takeover of so many aspects of the private economy has elicited so modulated a response. Yes, there have been tea parties, largely unreported, and there are town hall meetings over healthcare reform that have alarmed the administration with their ardor and anger. Nonetheless, the shift in the economy is nothing short of revolutionary.

Had this overreaching, this blatant attempt at government usurpation, occurred in another period Americans would have been out on the streets with pitchforks ready for combat. Most Americans, however, scarcely know what is happening. They don't get angry because they don't know what to be angry about. The primary issue that has seemingly captured attention is the proposed healthcare bill and its built-in constraints on personal freedom. I am still perplexed about the relatively modest protest. Perhaps the public doesn't know what is in the 1100-page bill- for that matter neither does the President nor the Congress. Perhaps the press has been complicit in the cover-up because it appears to be willing to take a vow of silence rather than embarrass President Obama. Perhaps restricting freedom doesn't mean what it once did. Perhaps Americans are so preoccupied with entertainment they haven't taken the time or made the effort to educate themselves.

It is certainly the case that young people are more likely to know the names of the four finalists on *American Idol* than four Cabinet members in the present administration. As I see it, there is a correlation between the preoccupation with amusement and the dumbing down of the population. If bread and circuses, or the contemporary equivalent, fill one's day, there simply isn't time for serious pursuits. If this seems exaggerated, ask how many serious words are exchanged in texting or how many ideas are explored on Facebook. Which magazine sells more copies, *The Star* or *Commentary*? The obvious answers reveal some aspect of the truth.

Of course, this is not to suggest that entertainment is wrong. It surely has a role in the culture at a time when critical, alas monumental, issues face the nation. One might assume that amusement would be relegated to a backseat, however temporary that condition might be. It seems as though the public is addicted to fun and games. Jay Leno, of late-night talk show fame, created a regular segment of his program making fun of undisguised ignorance. That ignorance is so penetrating that when I've seen it on display, I don't know whether to laugh or cry.

I should also note, before someone gets the wrong idea, that I am not supporting either revolution or a counterrevolution. I am simply eager to know why there hasn't been a public outcry loud enough to shake the Congress out of its perpetual stupor. I am also asking if the conditions that perpetuate a historical cycle of the kind identified by Sorokin are stifled by new, arguably ahistorical, conditions-namely, the ubiquity of amusement.

If my hypothesis is correct, it bodes poorly for the future. It is conceivable that the trade-off for continual entertainment is the incremental loss of personal liberty. That loss will be so subtle at first that it will hardly be recognized. When recognition does take place, it will be too late to undo the structural damage.

This contest between amusement and government intrusiveness and power accretion may be the most telling aspect of the Obama era. Will Americans wake up from the intoxication of sensate pleasure before liberty is lost? What a demonic question and what a potentially fearful and provocative response. There is little doubt that what we see and hear influences what we believe.

Kraft Foods representatives said that the company would stop advertising junk food to kids under 12. On January 12, 2005, the company issued a statement that such products as Oreos, Chips Ahoy, and most Oscar Mayer Lunchable meals would not be advertised on television, radio, or in print. The company claimed this was "a step in the right direction" in an effort to combat child obesity. It is instructive that Kraft's announcement came the same day the U.S. government issued its guidelines on appropriate dietary measures, which seem to suggest that Kraft was seeking to preempt government regulation of children's advertising.

More to the point is the interesting observation that what children see on television or popular media has an effect on how they act, an implicit admission in the Kraft Company statement. This claim is quite inconsistent with the argument of television executives who invariably argue that there is very little evidence that what young people watch is related to what they believe and how they behave.

The Kraft statement is merely one strand in an interlocking web of media presentations. The American Academy of Pediatrics has suggested that portrayals of sex on television-now the theme for 66 percent of prime time programs-may contribute to precocious adolescent sex. Empirical data examining the relationship is tentative and inadequate for addressing the issue of causation, but the evidence is still meaningful and suggestive.

Moreover, early sexual initiation is an important social and health issue. In fact, a recent survey indicates that most sexually experienced teens wished they had waited before their first sexual encounter. Almost all the data indicate that unplanned pregnancies and sexually transmitted diseases are far more common among those who begin sexual activity at any early age.

The conclusion of this American Academy report is that watching sex on TV predicts and may hasten adolescent sexual initiation. Reducing the amount of sexual content in entertainment programming, by contrast, could appreciably delay the initiation of coital and noncoital activity.

This, of course, is not the first study linking TV, sexual content, and attitudes to sex, including dissatisfaction with virginity and a whole range of perceptions regarding normative sexual initiation. This study, however, is among the most rigorous and careful ever conducted.

If one were to rely on the results of this study-and there appear to be valid reasons for doing so-the health hazards for adolescents from a regular diet of provocative sexual content on television programs are real and should not be discounted.

If such food companies as Kraft are sensitive to the relationship between advertising and obesity, television producers should be equally concerned between the relationship of prime time programming and its preoccupation with sex, including illegitimate births and the rate of teenage pregnancies in the United States.

Erstwhile mayor of New York Jimmy Walker once said "no one got pregnant from reading a book." My suspicion is Walker didn't read very much, and that he probably didn't read many salacious books. Of course, that is only an impression.

In a television age, however, nothing is left to the imagination. Programs deal with sex graphically and, in most instances, suggest directly or obliquely that sex at any age is desirable. That there may be a health hazard associated with adolescent sex is relegated to the dust bin of Puritanical behavior, a kind of Comstock critique.

It is remarkable that a disproportionate share of the 30 percent of children born out of wedlock has a teenage mother. It is true that in the last few years the rate of illegitimacy among teenage moms has declined slightly, but the leveling off has occurred at historically high rates, rates that suggest this is still a major health issue.

Lest someone contend this is a plea for censorship, let me nip that contention in the bud. The evidence seemingly suggests a plea for tastefulness and responsibility from television producers. Sex is an exciting and critical part of life, but it is only part of life. Just as Kraft Foods decided to forestall criticism with its own measures, it is high time television programmers did the same. *Sex and The City*, to cite one example, may be titillating, but it is far better for adults than for children. TV producers must learn that their responsibility is to a public trust, not only to a bottom line. Sex may sell, but it may destroy teenage lives as well.

Janet Jackson called it a wardrobe malfunction. Less delicate observers call it a strip. Whatever Justin Timberlake did when he ripped a piece off Janet Jackson's bustier costume, it certainly wasn't tasteful.

Most people observed yet another depredation in a media world grown coarse and grotesque. The way to get attention-who would deny that was the motive?-is to push the envelope to new and presumably more shocking levels.

Sexual innuendo has been pushed so far it is blatant. In fact, as previously stated "pornography is ubiquitous"-from ads that refer to "key exchanges" to miracle drugs that deal with erectile dysfunction. Family fare is suddenly sexual phantasmagoria.

For those who forgot or failed to notice, Michael Jackson, Janet's brother, held his crotch through a previous Super Bowl performance. Last year Madonna planted a sapphic kiss on Britney Spears for whatever shock value it might engender.

Viacom, which owns CBS, the network on which the game appeared, as well as MTV, which produced the half-time production, is also the company known for sponsoring lascivious and violent rap music that degrades the culture and poisons youthful minds.

F.C.C. chairman Michael Powell described the performance a "classless, crass, and deplorable stunt."[1] Of course he was right, but what he neglected to say was that the entire half-time show was crass and deplorable, from Kid Rock who desecrated the flag and used the requisite street language in his so-called music, to the talentless Justin Timberlake, who moved into Janet Jackson in simulated sexual motion.

Mr. Powell recently proposed action against Bono, lead singer for U2, who employed the "f word" while receiving an award during the live Golden Globes broadcast. In the end no action was taken because the context in which the word was used did not suggest indecency. What it does suggest is how deeply we are in the muck of moral decay.

In fact, most television programs, including those on primetime, are tasteless with sex being the overarching theme. It's as if TV producers feel a compulsion to compensate for the Puritanical views that once characterized the nation. Is it any wonder Americans are shock proof?

The level of general cultural degradation is now employed as a rationale for the perverse half-time Super Bowl show. Andy Rooney, CBS culture commentator, who I find neither funny nor insightful, said, "For what there is on television and in the entertainment industry these days, one bare breast doesn't seem like much to cause a fuss over." Well, that is precisely the point. American people are so immersed in smut that they are incapable of recognizing perversity even when in front of their eyes.

Because sex sells, it is sold 24/7. It is merely a commodity shouting for recognition.

CBS spokesman Chris Ender astonishingly argued: "The half topless escapade wasn't rehearsed, it wasn't discussed, it wasn't even hinted at." Janet Jackson, however, sees it differently.

She notes, "I decided after rehearsals to have a costume reveal." Because she decided, it was obviously her intention to shock the audience. Why didn't someone from CBS inquire about her intentions? Keep in mind Timberlake sang "I'll get you naked by the end of this song." Still, he contends the breast baring was "unintentional." Really?

Jackson's choreographer Gil Duldulao said, well before the event, there will be "shocking moments" in the half-time show. Alas, he knew what was coming. I suspect that CBS may have had prior knowledge as well. Who doesn't know what MTV productions are all about? Is it really surprising that sex was on center stage? Who is kidding whom?

Down the slippery slope of moral degradation we go. Where it stops nobody knows. One thing is certain: No matter how much controversy the Super Bowl half-time show fostered, it is virtually impossible to reverse the downward trajectory of Gresham's cultural law. Debasement is here and some of us now feel dirty watching a football game.

The half-time spectacle at the Super Bowl has finally alerted some members of the Congress to the depredations in popular culture; however, even this egregious event won't prepare most Americans for what is in store for them.

VH1 points out on its website that the station is engaged in an effort to link rock music and pornography. "Porn stars are seen as trophies, adding a coolness factor to a rock star's image. In the rap world, porn is another way rap stars can be entrepreneurs and make 'their paper.' The stars in each genre of music go about it differently but they all have learned that porn and porn stars are a 'GOOD thing'," notes the VH1 report.

Here is the devil's marriage: sex and perverse lyrics; rap and fornication. Wicked Girl Stephanie Swift is an aspiring singer. She is also one of Wicked Video's most popular porn stars. In her latest adult video, "Making It," Stephanie plays an aspiring singer who records a number of tracks that she combines with visual sex play.

Gene Simmons of Kiss is the publisher of *Tongue*, a magazine devoted to pornography. He is married to porn actress Shannon Tweed.

Barrett of rock band Dial 7, signed by Warner Bros., plays the bass and writes all the music. He has written two recent tracks about his fiancée Devon, a porn star, "Devon Stripped," and wrote the theme song for ESPN's new "extreme" show EXPN. By the way, he is also now performing in adult movies with Devon.

Snoop Dogg, who was featured on ads during the Super Bowl and who was profiled in the *NY Times Magazine*, has produced a tape, "Snoop's Doggystyle," that is part music video and part XXX film. He is in the rock vanguard now hosting the notorious *Girls Gone Wild* series which relies on hard core porn and rap music. In addition, he will soon be starring in the film, *Starsky and Hutch*.

Mystikal, the rapper known for the smash hit "Shake Ya Ass," teamed up recently with porn star Chace on the new album, *Liquid City*. A porn tape will be released with the album. The tape takes place at a record release party with partiers having sex in the club.

"Hip Hop Honeys" is a line of videos that features the notorious ladies of rap videos who talk frankly about sex and then do a striptease for the delectation of their fans.

Porn star Ron Jeremy has appeared in Kid Rock's video, "Cowboy," and went on tour with him. This is the same Kid Rock who sang at halftime during the Super Bowl wearing the American flag as an outer garment.

Digital Underground, known for the hit "The Humpty Dance," is also in the sex business. The group released the first adult sex and music video magazine designed to bring hip hop and pornography together. This magazine has five hardcore sex scenes along with uncensored interviews.

Although MTV and rap music have pushed the envelope to new levels of moral corruption, this is the first time popular music has been united with hard core pornography. What makes this even more pernicious than late night TV cable pornography is that the target audience is adolescents.

Smut sells. And the purveyors of this cultural poison only see dollar signs in their future. A culture that confuses liberty with libertine attitudes enables this condition to exist. At the moment, culture is unrestrained by moral boundaries.

Producers of smut know as much. They hide behind a latitudinarian interpretation of the First Amendment. Some judges, lacking a moral compass, confuse free expression with free speech and assume pornography should be protected like an editorial in the *New York Times*.

The effect of this extraordinary development in the world of rock music is easy to predict. Youthful expectations will be trapped in a swamp of perversity. Popular culture will evolve from sexual innuendo to outright, blatant sexual manifestations.

Whereas eroticism existed long before the present era, it hid appropriately in the crevices of hypocrisy. It could be purchased with a plain brown wrapper covering it, the tribute that vice paid virtue. That paper bag was the gossamer wedge between barbarism and civility. Its metaphorical power was profound.

The paper bag has now been torn and burned. There isn't any boundary separating barbarism from civilization. Youth cult is buying into perversity and the purveyors of pornography are both wealthy and popular, and they have entered the cultural mainstream.

Well before Janet Jackson and Kid Rock, Gene Simmons and Kiss performed at the 1999 Super Bowl. Snoop Dogg has become a megapersonality in the world of rap, claiming that he is a "reformed drug dealer" and a cultural exemplar.

In the world of rap, culture was gangsterized. It was a scenario similar to Thomas Mann's *Magic Mountain*[2], where those institutionalized came to manage the hospital. The sleazy side of life undermined the last vestige of decency. It is clear where this will end: the debasement of the society and the eradication of civility. Those making a fortune debilitating the young apparently simply do not care.

In an age where words meant whatever you chose to attribute to them, Andrea Fraser called herself an "artist." According to a *New York Times* article (6/13/04) Ms. Fraser videotaped a sexual encounter with an unidentified American "collector." This videotape is now being shown at the Friedrich Petzel Gallery in Chelsea. In it, Ms. Fraser demonstrated her artistic dexterity in "every imaginable position."

The consumer of her talents paid $20,000 for the artistic experience. Each segment of the filmed seduction was detailed in contractual terms before the "art" commenced. As Fraser explained, "All of my work is about what we want from art, what collectors want, what artists want from collectors, what museum audiences want." She is purportedly knowledgeable about wants.

She was not knowledgeable about art. As she saw it, selling art is prostitution, albeit when Baudelaire used this expression I don't think he meant it literally. Of course, in an art world that confuses sensation with aesthetics, Ms. Fraser had her defenders. Dan Cameron, curator at the New Museum, said: "Andrea's work has been about exposing the mechanism of the whole art system." It was not clear what system he was referencing.

Ms. Fraser was clearly not the first *soi disant* artist to use her body as a medium of expression. Examples abound. Perhaps the most illustrative was the purchase by the Tate Gallery of cans of feces from Piero Manzoni. In 2002 the gallery bought ninety tins of Manzoni's excrement for £22,300 British. This exceeds the price of gold by a wide margin. A spokesman for the gallery noted, "The Manzoni was a very important purchase for an extremely small amount of money; nobody can deny that." Well I can, but then my aesthetic judgment is limited.

By the way, the purchase was not the only excreta in the Tate collection. It also bought three paintings by Chris Ofili featuring elephant dung. This is the same artist who caused a sensation with his "Sensation" exhibit at the Brooklyn Museum several years ago.

As recent exhibits at the Whitney Museum demonstrated art and stunts are now indistinguishable. Ms. Fraser's video, entitled "Untitled," should have been called XXX porn if there were truth in advertising. Critics instead called this pornography "transgressive art" or "interactive art." Interactive indeed.

Ms. Fraser claims her work was designed to lampoon the pretentious critique of art and the cult of museum worshippers who stared at tins of excrement as if it's a Da Vinci painting; however, this mimicry has gone to a new level. Now she is not a person, but a work of art. Alas, this is a claim anyone can make-a claim Ms. Fraser would probably embrace in the era of peoples' art.

At the end of the *New York Times* piece Ms. Fraser confessed that she is fearful about the anonymous collector. After all, his reputation might be exposed and damaged. It would appear that there is very little that can be done to affect her reputation.

Now if only one could blast through the haze of artistic babble, this art should be called a transaction. It is sex for sale at a very high price. She is a hooker and the collector is a john. Thousands of people may have this transaction in motels around the country, but none of them confuse fornication with art.

The remarkable thing was that the paper of record has any story about Ms. Fraser as an artist. Have we reached a stage of degradation where sex and art have blurred our consciousness? Is it the price that made it an art form or the video tape? And what can Ms. Fraser do for an encore?

If one wondered whether art suffers from aesthetic exhaustion, one needed look no further than Ms. Fraser's work. The idea that an artist requires discipline and talent has been replaced by the notion that anyone who chooses to call himself an artist and is willing to shock the public with self-deprecatory acts is a designated artist.

That a portion of the public is taken in by this absurdity reminds us that the fable of an emperor without clothes lives in the modern museums of America. Mountebanks are born every minute and now many choose to call themselves artists.

Marcelee Gralapp, the library director of the Boulder Colorado Public Library very recently refused to display an American flag. She gave as her reason the belief that a flag would compromise the library's objectivity. After a number of protests Ms. Gralapp relented by placing a small flag on a pole at the library entrance.

A week after this incident Ms. Gralapp put twenty-one sculptures on display in the library art gallery. The exhibit was called "Hung Out To Dry." In it ceramic penises were hung from knitted cozies clothes-pinned to a cord strung between a wall and a column. One end of the cord is tied to a noose.

Boulder spokesman Jana Peterson asked, how can you balk at showing the American flag but think it's appropriate to display ceramic penises? Good question, for which there wasn't a response.

The *Rocky Mountain News* (11/8/01[3]) reported that an unidentified mother said to her son who was staring at the exhibit, "No dear, they're corn cobs."

What they are of course is bad taste. This event perhaps most significantly suggests something about the degradation of taste for those who can confuse shock value with artistic expression.

What then is the relationship between the flag and the depraved art exhibit? Although I can only surmise, I think there is a relationship.

For many radicals the American flag embodies everything they hate. It is the embodiment of racism, colonialism, class consciousness, and the commodification of culture. The hate-America crowd views the flag as bourgeois culture, the detestable middle class and its provincial values.

By contrast, avant-garde art decries the bourgeoisie. The art is designed to shock the middle class from its provincialism. Its aesthetic position-to the extent it has one-is challenge at every turn.

Needless to say, the Marcelee Gralapps are in a small minority, made even smaller since September 11, yet it is instructive that a small minority can have a profound effect on public opinion, especially if it is recognized. Ms. Gralapp represents a public institution, one supported by taxpayer funding. Her actions have received attention in large part because the library is a public institution. Had the exhibit been organized in a private gallery, it would certainly not be a matter of public debate.

It is ironic that the flag-a symbol of liberty-was not flown because it would compromise objectivity, yet the display of objectionable art protected by that liberty is a condition of which the librarian readily took advantage. It has surely not occurred to her that the symbol of the flag protects artistic expression.

Even in Boulder, sometimes thought of as Moscow West, the Gralapp position is not acceptable. University towns, however, do have a gravitational pull for disgruntled leftists.

I would hope that at some point Ms. Gralapp might be asked to defend her position. The radical stance invariably is that tastelessness is permitted in a free society, but that argument presupposes the existence and defense of freedom. Whether Ms. Gralapp agrees, the stars and stripes represent that liberty.

If anything should be "hung out to dry" it is patently absurd arguments that are neither defensible nor sensible, yet that, too, is an outcome liberty affords. Of course, it should be noted that the excess of liberty is license, a distinction lost on a previous generation.

It is instructive that the fortieth anniversary of Woodstock has passed and, with it, the romantic remembrances of days past. One program after another has described the musical encounters, the unfettered expression, and even the mud and grime as the beginning of a "new age." Woodstock has taken on the mantle of a generational theme. Millions claim to have been among the estimated crowd of 400,000.

Ang Lee has taken advantage of this nostalgic journey with his film, *Taking Woodstock*, albeit there isn't any attempt to describe the music at this event. That's probably just as well because most youthful adherents weren't listening to the music and many of those who did were too high to know what they were experiencing.

I have another view of Woodstock. A self-indulgent generation weaned on the slogan better living through chemistry sought to display unfettered expression on a cow pasture in New York State. All the romanticized hogwash cannot rationalize youngsters hooked on drugs, sex, and rock and roll. Most were simply riding the Eden express to a place called oblivion. They weren't committed to "new ideas," as if there are any, nor were they revolutionaries; they simply wanted to have fun.

To superordinate this youthful venture in rebellion to some kind of religious awakening is absurd on any level, including the debased level of the revelers. It is remarkable that as the years pass and the baby boomer generation wears its graying pony tails to Grateful Dead concerts, Woodstock has taken on a quasi-religious designation. For many, a roll in the hay is recalled as a roll in the mud, a moment when you could let it all hang out because anything goes was the *modus operandi*.

This was undisguised bacchanalia, nothing more or less. Why convert it into the Great Awakening of the Sixties? If anything, it was designed to shock an already shockproof America. It was giving the finger to bourgeois society by the children of the bourgeoisie. These weren't poor kids trapped in the inner city of marginal schools and insufficient jobs. These were the progeny of privilege acting out in a town far from home with kindred souls who found the liberating effects of drugs.

After all, drugs were the lubricant for antisocial expression. They reduced the barriers established by the super-ego. In effect, they said "if it feels good, do it." For some, the drugs offered freedom; for others, it gave a jolting kick in the rear as overdoses and vomiting were a reminder reality hadn't evanesced. Brain cells were damaged by drug-addled youths who didn't know when to stop or who thought they could defy gravity on LSD.

Sure, one can look back and say it was a remarkable event, a gathering unlike others. There is some truth to this claim, but this is a marginal truth, the footnote to a real story. The existential truth is that a lot of youngsters eager to overcome restrictions demanded by social norms found an outlet at Woodstock. These weren't revolutionaries, although they claimed that title. They were merely rationalizing behavior their parents reproved.

Before Woodstock is given a chapter heading in American history, it behooves those who can remember without the assistance of rose colored glasses to tell the actual story. That is the story of wild orgies, drug-fueled memories and filth-port-o-potties that didn't work, mounds of vomit, and excrement that was ground into the soil as fertilizer.

For those too young to know, beware of claims about Woodstock. It was not all it was cracked up to be and it certainly is not deserving of nostalgic praise. Memories, of course, can play tricks on us. As I see it, Woodstock is among the most elaborate tricks of all. Of course it is not the only trick played on us

Gambling as a source of revenue enhancement is yet another government trick.

It was humid on the Atlantic City boardwalk, but inside the gambling casinos the air was cool and smoky. Thousands of tourists filled the beach hotels for air conditioning, entertainment, and, most important of all, gambling.

Everyone in Atlantic City thinks they can strike it rich. Little old ladies from Sheepshead Bay took the bus ride of 120 miles to find the pot of gold at the end of the rainbow. A young businessman from Mac Arthur Avenue in the Bronx was searching for the "big hit" at the blackjack tables. By the way, he sat at the $100 table. Patrick Ewing, once of the New York Knicks, sat alone at the Caesar's baccarat table hoping to enhance his former multimillion dollar salary.

If asked, each in turn would call this fun. Perhaps it was. I am not so paternalistic as to believe I should tell others what to enjoy. There was a desperation, however, that surrounded the casino.

When people lose more than they can afford, sadness colors their appearance. The lines at the ATM machines are manifestations of a need to continue even when the results are disappointing.

One found the tortured logic that one can beat the odds heavily stacked in favor of the house. Here is the triumph of hope over reality.

Sure, there is the occasional winner; the house must provide incentives for hope to remain alive. By and large, Atlantic City is an inverted Robin Hood scheme in which the poor give to the rich. The porter playing the slots is making a financial transfer to Donald Trump.

At the blackjack table a young black man in his twenties drew another card on 17 even though the dealer is showing an exposed 6, which means he will probably have to take another card. In this case, the odds of the dealer going over 21 are high. The young man defies the odds and loses even though the dealer does go over 21 and other players rejoice. Fifty dollars disappear. I wonder how long it took this young fellow to earn $50. I wonder as well whether this is entertaining for him.

My view of this gambling phenomenon was colored by experience. I know how hard most people work to earn $50. I know as well that casinos are not in business to give money away, yet for many the lure is irresistible.

The old women sat transfixed staring at bars and cherries in a slot machine. Their cups were filled with coins; the house started them out with $10 in quarters. They guarded their positions jealously, pulling the lever with gusto hoping that, just maybe, hundreds of quarters would fall into their laps.

That occasionally happens. They would let out a yelp and go back to the one-armed bandit. By the end of the day-when the buses are loaded to take them back to New York City-most of their paper cups were empty. Some will say this was merely an outing; many, of course, are addicted.

Some lied to their friends indicating a net return on investment. Most, however, are philosophical: "I lost, but I enjoyed myself." I wonder.

Most of the people I observed didn't seem happy. Some were desperate; many were disconsolate and a few, flush with victory, were joyous. This was merely another day in Atlantic City where the gamblers never leave and the proprietors always win.

Gambling has clearly allowed Atlantic City to make a comeback from the doldrums of decay and sleaziness, but the price is high. Without moralizing, there is no doubt that this city of temptation puts many lives on the line. Families are sometimes put at risk and, in truth, gambling is only a transfer arrangement, not a generator of wealth.

In appealing to the human aspiration for easy success, Atlantic City is a giant lottery, a place where unrealistic dreams are fostered. In a moment of sobriety you can unfortunately see the losers crying in alcoves and the lost souls on side streets. This is the other side of Atlantic City the glitz conceals.

There is virtually no end to lunacy for a portion of the brain-dulled public. Those afflicted with a radical sensibility rarely find humor in their actions, but funny and pathetic responses usually emanate from the well of ideological gesturing. Even popular culture isn't immune to this condition.

When I was a kid and an avid consumer of Superman comics, I would look up in the sky and say to my playmates, "It's a bird, it's a plane, no, it's Superman." I would then pretend to fly away with the cape my mom made for me flapping in the wind.

I wasn't a *uber menchen* of the Nietzschian variety; in fact, the only Nietzsche I knew played middle linebacker for the Green Bay Packers. But I was obsessed with Superman. After all, he had a secret identity as fledgling reporter and he had Lois Lane, in what appeared to be unrequited love.

I was reminded of this because of the opening of the much heralded film, *Superman Returns*. Here was my chance to revisit atavistic yearnings. Needless to say, technical marvels are evident throughout the movie. The Christopher Reeve look-a-like was a passable Superman and Kate Bosworth as Lois is terrific.

I have a gripe, in fact, a major gripe. The screenwriters have committed a transgression that is simply inexcusable. Superman's motto, "Truth, justice and the American way" has been rewritten to, "Truth, justice and …all that stuff." "All that stuff!"

In the era of political correctness, the screenwriters obviously wanted to avoid the charge of jingoism. As Mike Dougherty, one of the screenwriters, explained, "He's not just for Metropolis and not just for America."[4] Mr. Dougherty's colleague Dan Harris elaborates, "He's an alien from Krypton; he has come to Earth to be kind of a savior for this world, not our country… And he has no papers."

Superman's enemy, Lex Luthor, is admittedly intent on creating a new continent that might serve as a rationalization for the politically correct motto, but I am upset that the new Superman, like most of his Hollywood creators, has been converted into a transnationalist. I suspect that in a sequel Superman will be employed by the United Nations.

A politically correct Superman will soon be asked to establish his miraculous feats on an affirmative action schedule. Of course, the sport he plays is soccer, excuse me, I should have said "football."

Could it be that the producers were concerned about ticket sales in anti-American settings like France? In the past Superman would have said "Je ne suis pas francais," or words that are less polite.

Superman was invented here; he is ours. Raised on a Midwestern farm, he is distinctly American. He came to Metropolis, not to Paris. It doesn't make sense to internationalize Superman, even if he came from a distant planet.

On one level this is a silly exegesis into popular and adolescent fare. As recent history would suggest, symbol matters. Is the flag merely cloth dyed in red, white, and blue? Is the Red Cross the residue of a Rorschach test?

Superman is a symbol of extraordinary actions, actions-I should note-that only the United States can perform. If the day comes when American military forces are obliged to wear a U.N. insignia, the United States' stature on the world stage will be in decline.

I think the Superman of my youth should be disinterred. He should fight for the American way; he should change his red, blue, and yellow outfit for the red, white and blue. He should tell Lois Lane-like Dorothy in The Wizard of Oz-"there's no place like home."

We don't need a man of tin; Superman is the man of steel whose steely resistance to evil is the aim of American policy, notwithstanding the critics who harp on government blunders, mistakes, and imperfections. Superman is the popular exemplar of the American creed. He is the American popular hero: humble, brave, and resourceful.

How dare the Hollywood radicals convert him into a symbol of their misguided vision.

Chapter 4
False Prophets

We often believe that media characterizations are real, but in the process of accepting false notions, the distinction between the actual and the mythical is blurred.

Although I have maintained a personal policy of not criticizing those who have passed this mortal coil, recent events have forced me to modify my position. Media outlets of every kind have gone through an orgy of admiration for three fallen Americans: Senator Ted Kennedy, Walter Cronkite, and Michael Jackson. Based on the continual coverage of these three men, you would have assumed they were candidates for beatification.

This media festival overlooked what press myrmidons often overlook; namely, how flawed each of these people were. How can one overlook Mary Jo Kopechne, the young lady whose life was cut short by the senator's desire to maintain his reputation? How can one overlook the insidious role of Mr. Cronkite in undermining the American war effort in Vietnam? How can one excuse the drug addled, pedophilia of Michael Jackson?

That isn't to say these people didn't have modest accomplishments; but these were accomplishments bounded by flaws-deep-seated flaws. The reason to mention this matter is that a nation needs heroes, people to admire and emulate. Whatever one thinks about these three men, they are not heroes-notwithstanding overblown eulogies-and they are certainly not worthy of emulation.

One of the nation's problems is that false prophets are easily superordinated into heroes by the exaggerated claims of media moguls. One observes the magnification of modest achievement into full-blown adoration. The famous who are cult figures are conflated with the infamous. In fact, there is scarcely a distinction between the two words.

This raises the curious question of who does one admire in a society and culture that puts a premium on being well known? The anonymous person working in a hospice to assist the terminally ill is in my judgment a genuine hero. That person, however, will not receive a television funeral when he or she passes from this life. How does one decide who to admire when the air waves tell us that a celebrity, however flawed, is worthy of our respect?

I for one do not respect Kennedy, Cronkite, and Jackson. If anything, the public tributes have left me with an empty feeling that our culture is adrift in mediocrity, sophistry, and relativism. It seems as if we cannot distinguish between heroes and frauds, the famous and infamous, the self-indulgent and the magnanimous. The spirit of a nation is sapped by the obsession with marginal people elevated to the heights of Mount Olympus thralldom.

At Kennedy's funeral service President Obama compared Kennedy with Daniel Webster, as the two greatest senators in American history. This hyperbole may be understandable since former presidents and the Kennedy family were in attendance, but on a serious level the claim is ludicrous. Webster was among the most gifted speakers the Senate has ever had. Kennedy demonstrated a halting and ineffective pattern of speech. Webster had a brilliant and fertile mind. Kennedy, by any standard, was a marginal and predictable thinker.

In the age of false prophets, you can get away with these comparisons. The public rarely knows the full story and, by and large, doesn't care to know. Jackson will be remembered for the *Thriller* album and his "moonwalk"; Cronkite for his mellifluous voice and sign-off. Is that enough to put them in the pantheon of heroes? When we do so, what harm do we cause those who genuinely deserve heroic status-the young men who gave their lives defending the nation; the tireless workers who maintain national prosperity; the hospital attendants who tend to the sick.

America is exceptional because so many labor in anonymity to help others. As I see it, these are the real heroes, the ones who should be famous through example, not the false prophets who are merely overblown characters on a television screen. In fact, it is the inversion of truth that sets us back, that invades the vineyards of principle and values.

The search for truth has curiously been compromised by intimidation. In what can only be described as a perplexing review Lorraine Adams, *New York Times Book Review* (12/14/08), examines *The Jewel of Medina*, the Sherry Jones novel about the Prophet Mohammed and his marriage to the nine year old A'isha. Employing a sneering tone, Ms. Adams skewers the book as "historical romance," a swipe recognizable to the cognoscenti.

What makes the review notable is that Random House, the original publisher, refused to issue the book on the grounds it would offend the Muslim community and might result in a violent reaction. As a consequence, this decision planted the novel squarely in a free speech controversy.

Ms. Adams seems to suggest that since the novel doesn't have literary merit, the Random House decision was appropriate, notwithstanding the fact that officials at the publishing house did not use merit or lack thereof as a reason to suspend publication.

Ms. Adams employs a form of moral equivalence in her review suggesting that both *Satanic Verses*[1] and Martin Scorsese's film *Last Temptation of Christ* resulted in violent reaction from Muslim and Christian communities. It is presumed that when religious groups are offended by an unflattering presentation of doctrine or prophets, violence results.

This judgment, however, is skewed in an unrecognizable direction. Although there was an incident that resulted from the showing of the *Last Temptation of Christ*, it is difficult, alas implausible, to contend that Christians engage in violent behavior when Jesus is besmirched or Church doctrine is violated. In fact, Dan Brown's *DaVinci Code*[2] also promoted the blasphemous idea that Jesus married Mary Magdalene, but I could not find any evidence of violence against the book or the film. Criticism, yes; violence, no.

Contrast that stand, with the consistent pattern of violence when Muslims are offended. In fact, to suggest that the two religious responses to offense are comparable enters the realm of the absurd. Quoting a professor of Islamic history at the University of Texas Ms. Adams notes, "I don't have a problem with historical fiction. I do have a problem with the deliberate misinterpretation of history. You can't play with a sacred history and turn it into soft-core pornography."

Well, yes, you can, as Dan Brown demonstrated. Moreover, even well-meaning professors of Islamic studies do not know the full story of the Prophet Mohammed and A'isha. Why isn't Ms. Jones entitled to poetic license in a novel?

Because Lorraine Adams cannot defend Random House's imposition on free speech, she contends "Jones' prose is lamentable" and adds that "an inexperienced, untalented author has naively stepped into an intense and deeply sensitive intellectual argument." When did it become unacceptable for an author to step into a sensitive intellectual argument?

One doesn't have to applaud Ms. Jones' effort to approve of the publication of her book. Nor does one have to regard it as art in order to countenance publication. I am often astonished at the trash that makes the *New York Times* best seller list.

As a final fillip Ms. Adams notes, "It is telling that PEN, the international association of writers that works to advance literature and defend free expression has remained silent on the subject of the novel." Could it be that PEN is also intimidated by the prospect of violence? Might PEN be so inured to political correctness that it only defends free expression when it happens to be consonant with prevailing sentiments at this august body?

Ms. Adams has delivered another in a long line of patronizing reviews in the Book Review section, but this one, in my opinion, crosses the line of fair play. It is of little consequence whether Jones has written a masterpiece or a historical romance. After all, historical romances do get published. It is noteworthy, however, that a writer at the *Times* has attempted to justify censorship using a qualitative standard of her preferences and relegating violence to an incidental concern of the Random House officials. No wonder many of us think free speech is imperiled. The manipulation of truth, from which freedom emerges, has become a cottage industry.

Some people never learn despite all the evidence put before them. James Gustave Speth, the dean of the Yale School of Forestry and Environment Studies, appears to be one of these people.

Writing in the *International Herald Tribune*[3] Professor Speth contends that the Global 2000 Report to the president, in which he played a part, was "frighteningly on target." He notes:

> Most people will soon live in water-stressed areas. Half the tropical forests are gone. Bird and mammal species are disappearing at a rate 100 to 1000 times the rate at which extinction naturally occur. Seventy percent of marine fisheries are either fished to capacity or overfished. Most threatening of all, global climate change is well under way.

Here is the litany of gloomy and doomsayer predictions that characterized the Carter administration and remain alive and well in a segment of the environmental community. Moreover, Professor Speth and his colleagues invariably go through predictable lamentations about the "terrible Bush administration" that has not embraced the Kyoto Accord and the woefully inadequate funding for environmental catastrophes just around the corner.

Ending his article with a Cassandra-like flourish Speth writes "The alarms sounded twenty years ago have not been heeded, and soon it will be too late to prevent an appalling deterioration of the natural world."

Let's consider a variety of facts Professor Speth chooses to ignore.

By the end of the twentieth century it was already clear that most forms of pollution that alarm ecopessimists were in decline. Even nitrogen oxide is on a downward trend after increasing between 1970 and 1980.

Whereas CO_2 concentrations have grown, their effect on climate is not clear. Climate data over the last 100 years or so show no consistent correlation with CO_2 accumulations. In fact, average global temperatures were higher 1000 years ago than they are today, at a time when very little manmade CO_2 was emitted.

Major air pollutant emissions have declined by 60 percent in the United States from their peak in the 1950s. Worldwide per capita emissions of CO_2, the main concern of global warming theorists, appear to have peaked in the late 1970s.

Moreover, the search for alternatives to fossil fuels has accelerated with nuclear energy plants, natural gas, photovoltaic cells, hydrogen-powered fuel cells, and hybrid car engines fast becoming cost-effective alternatives.

Species disappearance is yet another unjustified, and perhaps unjustifiable, claim. Because only a tiny fraction of flora and fauna species has been identified it is hard to know the pace of disappearance-if indeed disappearance is occurring at all. Nature, after all, is engaged in its own form of creative destruction, as the disappearance of the dinosaurs can attest.

A significant error of the ecopessimists-modern day Malthusians-is the extrapolation of the future from the immediate past. The successful transformation of nature to the benefit of humanity is likely to continue, notwithstanding many of technology's disadvantages.

The genius of mankind resides in its ability to adapt, and it is precisely that adaptational ability that will ensure preservation of the environment. It is surely not ordained by any iron law of history that economic expansion will occur. An unlimited array of options stand before us, but it is important to realize that people are not lemmings, poised at the edge of a cliff they don't jump off.

Environmental conditions are within our control. First, we must act responsibly and dispassionately. Second we must remember that guarded optimism is a more realistic guide to the future than paralytic pessimism. Were it up to the ecopessimists air conditioners, cars, and heavy manufacturing would not exist. We would return to the Stone Age when the air and water were perfectly pure.

The problem is most people today don't want to live in the world of 5000 years ago.

On September 24, 2007, Vaclav Klaus[4], the president of Czech Republic, addressed the U.N. General Assembly on global warming. This was a speech Al Gore probably received with alarm if he heard it at all. Klaus maintained that the essence of global warming is not understood and the campaign Gore has promoted is wildly inconsistent with the evidence.

President Klaus is not alone in his assessment. According to Fred Singer[5], professor emeritus of Climatology at University of Virginia, there are 500 scientists who agree in one way or another with Klaus, notwithstanding the fact that one *60 Minutes* reporter claimed denying the reality of global warming is comparable to "Holocaust denial."

Because science is subject to hypothesis, testing, and evaluation, there are facts that can be analyzed and, even if disagreements emerge, debate and discussion should be possible. This is simply not the case when it comes to global warming.

The Heartland Institute ran ads in the major national newspapers inviting Al Gore to debate Lord Moncton, Lady Thatcher's science adviser, Dennis Avery[6], co-author of *Unstoppable Global Warming*, and the previously mentioned Vaclav Klaus. But Mr. Gore was nowhere to be found.

Despite Gore's contention that scientific evidence for global warming is incontrovertible, there are many who believe the science for this claim is unsettled.

The question is whether proponents of global warming have an agenda or whether they are merely dispassionate purveyors of scientific evidence. Discussion, debate, and open dialogue might presumably help to address this issue, but Gore is not rising for the bait.

One detractor, Dennis Avery, argues that recent weather history is consistent with 600 previous warming periods in the last million years. He contends that the Earth has gone through many warming and cooling cycles based on the sun's temperature variation and its influence on our pla net.

Lord Moncton[7], who did exchange views with Gore on the pages of the *Sunday Telegraph* in 2006, contends he has rather "half-baked, jumbled, and prodigiously exaggerated notions." Moncton, with several other well-known analysts, maintains that taking Gore's position seriously would lead inexorably to a severe misallocation of resources and would ultimately have a catastrophic effect.

The Gore campaign, however, has an ineluctable momentum about it fueled in large part by Hollywood adherents eager to posture themselves as global saviors and media panjandrums who believe (rightly, I might add) that global warming has entered the national consciousness as a problem that must be addressed.

Lurching to address a problem without sufficient understanding of it, however, can have deleterious consequences. Moreover, the two most populous nations in the world, India and China, which account for at least a third of the earth's population, will not consider carbon limits that inhibit their extraordinary industrial and technical growth.

Then what might be done? First and foremost, all the theories and known evidence should be made transparent. U.N. statistics often employed as the standard for global warming proponents should be put under the glare of careful examination. Competing positions should be aired.

Last, Mr. Gore, who has been canonized by Hollywood, should attempt to defend *An Inconvenient Truth*, his film about global warming, in front of a panel of disinterested scientists. The Heartland Institute set down the challenge: If Gore feels so strongly about his position, he should be able to defend it in front of critics. If he is reluctant to do so, one cannot help but wonder whether any of his claims are valid.

This challenge suggests that clichés and epithets are not a substitute for genuine thought. My own experience often brought home this obvious conclusion.

In 1994, during my campaign for New York State Comptroller against Carl McCall, the race card was played persistently by members of the press and by my opponent. Because I had been active in civil rights causes, opened a headquarters in Harlem, was a sponsor of CORE events, and had two men of color as my campaign chairmen, Reuben Diaz and Roy Innis, I was perplexed and disappointed. It became exceedingly ugly when Bob Herbert in a *New York Times* column called me a "racist," a claim that was made without the slightest effort to speak to me directly or examine my record.

Even though I thought I was emotionally calloused the charge hurt. It most significantly had a chastening influence on my campaign. Even though I felt Mr. McCall made mistakes in our debates and had adopted positions that made him vulnerable to criticism, I was reluctant to challenge him. It was restraint borne of a false, but effective charge.

As I listened to comments by former President Jimmy Carter and other members of the Democratic party, I have had a strange sense of déjà vu. Some have argued that criticism of the president's healthcare proposal is based on race, not the weakness in the proposed legislation. If you accept this argument, criticism is negated by its egregious and prejudicial character. President Obama presumably wants to move the country ahead, but the contemporary Bull Connors have plotted to undermine his effort.

It is one thing for an irresponsible radio personality like Janeane Garafalo to make this outrageous claim, but when it is made by leaders in the party, the effect can be chilling. It means that bullying tactics can be used to stifle debate. Race will both be employed as a trump card, and it will be the catalyst for dictatorial control.

Should criticism hit home, arguments that cannot be rationally countered will be neutralized with the "nuclear race option." Serious proponents of Obamacare must surely realize that well-meaning critics can differ with the president on the essential features and details of his proposal, but it is easy to challenge reflexively using race as the *sine qua non* of argumentation.

For a president who said he was committed to a postracial administration, it would make sense for him to repudiate this stratagem. He has been either conspicuously silent on this matter, or insulting to his critics. In a way that may indeed be inadvertent, he is promoting the use of the race card as a political device.

It is instructive that the more argumentation reverts to this base ploy, the less value it has. The racist charge has lost its effect because of the irresponsible manner in which it's employed. I can recall Rep. Charlie Rangel maintaining that tax cuts were a function of racism. Every police action against a black assailant was invariably a racist act according to the Reverend Al Sharpton. Companies that did not support Reverend Jesse Jackson's foundation were *ipso facto* racist organizations.

The public is increasingly desensitized to this extortion racket, but it is quite another matter when the president's adherents rely on white guilt to buttress their position. This stance is divisive and dangerous. Stifling debate is not the sort of thing a president can encourage without deep-seated damage to the body politic.

I have been on the receiving end of this tactic and can testify it isn't pretty. I won't say it isn't fair because that is obvious; however, with some- and I fall into this category-it is effective. Once you start engaging in preemptive censorship, the other side of the debate has won even if his position is flimsy and unworthy.

It is time to put race to bed, to realize it should neither be an advantage nor a disadvantage. For race baiters, however, that is impossible; it is all they know and the one tactic that has yielded the result they want. If President Obama is intent on bringing Americans together, he must denounce this ploy once and for all even if it means his detractors are free to challenge his proposals. After all, these challenges could make his arguments stronger than they are at the moment, and might even be good for the soul of the nation.

There is little doubt that the French are enthralled with President Obama. The presumption is that a new era in Franco-American relations has been launched. Because it is too early to assess the president's policies, I have asked my French friends what accounts for their enthusiasm. Although the comments vary, there is a central theme: A man of color will lead us forward.

Despite the sincerity of this claim, I find it curious. On the one hand, commentators on both sides of the Atlantic argue that Obama has ushered in a postracial period in which racial attitudes are irrelevant; however, they also suggest that the color of his skin is critical in the assessment of his presidency.

Needless to say, hypocrisy is not restricted to the Obama presidency; however, black celebrities who have been interviewed invariably say that at long last they can believe in a president and now they "have come to love America" (vide: Beyonce). A black American or for that matter an Algerian residing in France presumably couldn't admire an American president or the nation until a man of color became president.

It is one thing to identify racial pride, but the attitude on display suggests that many Americans deriving all the benefit and privileges the United States confers did not appreciate or understand these conditions until a black man was elected president.

Either this suggests remarkable ignorance or a willful disregard for the unique qualities America possesses. American liberty wasn't born with Obama. Moreover, despite errors in the past and the mistreatment of blacks through a substantial portion of the national history, politicians in both parties have attempted to redress the wrong of the past over the last half century.

History did not begin with Bill Clinton, did not cease with George W. Bush, and was not resuscitated with Barack Obama. That remarkably is not the way the Obama era is being treated.

Every French bookstore has books on Obama prominently displayed. His picture is far more prominent in France than President Sarkozy. In fact, every breath the new American president takes is recorded for posterity. This fascination with Obama has reached ridiculous proportions.

Some French commentators rather patronizingly say it is about time Americans had a black president. I usually greet this comment with a question: When will France have an Algerian president or perhaps one from Cote d'Ivoire? My question is usually met with silence accompanied by a frown.

As I see it, the Obama election demonstrates how far we've progressed and how little we've progressed. On one level, Americans can elect a president notwithstanding his race. On another level, race was an overarching factor in his election and in his international standing.

Suppose for the sake of argument, Obama serves two terms and is succeded by Eric Holder, the Attorney General-designate who is also black. In sixteen years a teenager at the moment will have known only black presidents during this formative period in his political life. Would teens in the middle of 2024 suggest that its time we had a white president? Would they note that they couldn't appreciate the quality of American liberty until a white man were elected to the highest office in the land? On any level these questions are absurd, but are they any more absurd than the chant echoing through contemporary life that America can finally be appreciated because a black man has been elected? Is race-either as a positive or negative-a national obsession? Isn't it time we gave it a rest and truly got beyond the racial question completely.

Albert Camus[8] was expert at describing a man apart, an existential man-*The Stranger*-who didn't belong in the society in which he found himself. He didn't have emotional roots; in fact, this character was haunted by shadows-the real and the metaphorical. He is the quintessential rebel challenging normative standards.

At the risk of drawing literary comparisons, I am persuaded based on his performance that President Obama is a man apart. He seems to equate power with arrogance; pride with willfulness, and exceptionalism with dominance. As a consequence, he has changed foreign policy perceptions. The America he leads is a nation like any other-no more, no less. In fact, as a Nobel laureate, he is considered by the Europeans as a man of the world, not merely a citizen of the United States.

When asked if the United States is exceptional, President Obama said America is exceptional and England is exceptional and Greece is exceptional. That the United States is *sui generis* didn't cross his mind. How could it? He is pledged to a scenario in which America opts out of its traditional role as peacekeeper, the balance wheel in maintaining international equilibrium. The war against terrorists is over along with the nation's hegemonic role.

The war fatigue President Obama embodies is unfortunately not embraced by our global enemies who see this shift in his policy attitude as a sign of weakness and retreat. I believe President Obama actually thinks that unilateral concessions to our real and putative enemies will result in reciprocal responses, but as his bizarre overtures to the Olympic Committee demonstrated, gestures directed at multilateralism and celebrity status do not result in favorable results. Real power as opposed to soft power still has meaning on the world stage.

A man with roots would know that wild policy swings of the kind that we've experienced with healthcare, cap and trade, and education proposals cannot possibly fly with the American people, even with those who voted for President Obama in the last election. Despite cultural shifts in the nation, the United States still fashions itself as a conservative nation. Only a man apart cannot sense that condition.

My contention is not that the president is devoid of conviction. In fact, his political tilt is decidedly to the left, the hardcore left. My assertion is different. I believe this president doesn't understand the rhythms, the pulse of the American people. He is not merely outside the main stream. He doesn't even recognize it. He is a basketball player who has been asked to bat.

At first I thought his initial popularity would carry him through to a second term. As each day passes and the false, almost inappropriate, gestures register, however, Americans are beginning to recognize this man apart. He is our stranger in a land he doesn't understand.

Americans are not warlike, nor does imperial ambition fill their soul. They have done almost nothing for which daily apologies are necessary. Their blood soaks the beaches of Normandy, their graves litter European towns. Their fortune saved millions from the plight of destitution. Americans do not appreciate a man so removed from their history, so out of tune with the American experience, that he reflexively expresses regret for the very conditions that should engender pride.

Perhaps this president will learn. I am not confident that can happen. His life experience without a father in his home and a mother seeking adventure abroad is unstable. His closest associates vilified the nation he now leads. Is it any wonder his wife said she could take no pride in America till now? The past is to be rejected. Milestones in history are erased from memory as storage cast aside as unnecessary.

This is a unique moment in our history. It is certainly the only time in my life when our national instincts are being reconditioned. From a nation that was a model to the world, we are now told that superiority is unbecoming, a hindrance for the emergence of global egalitarianism.

President Obama, as a man apart, may attempt this recasting of America, but, as I see it, America is not yet ready for his experimentation and, most likely, never will be.

Chapter 5
Technology Is Creating A Brave or Foolish New World

Technology is here because it is here, but the use and abuse in our lives is unclear.

It is a virtual cliché born of overstatement to suggest the world is interconnected. Technology has created the information economy and according to Thomas Friedman[1], has made "the world flat." The p.c. has presumably made decisions possible in real time, has offered opportunities for labor, commerce and wealth production on an unprecedented scale, and provided benefits too numerous to identify. Let me illustrate.

Most libraries will soon be book-free and devoid of people. In the cyberspace age most research is done online. Google is in the throes of digitizing 32 million books on its site. For the Google entrepreneurs, content hasn't any value. It is the viewer who is important, the person who wants the content. Needless to say, for authors this may appear as copyright infringement, but for the researcher it is nirvana.

Any topic the mind can conjure is or will soon be researchable. Buildings housing books have become places for repose or for codgers like me who love dusty stacks. The library of books and archives, is quickly becoming an anachronism.

A technology that transmits information in words and pictures similarly can advise and educate. A surgeon at NYU hospital can assist with a surgery in Nairobi; a grandma in New Jersey can provide visual evidence for her cold remedy to a grandchild in Los Angeles.

Behavioral targeting, to wit: The preferences of online users are collected and offered to advertisers capable of targeting individual consumers. "Deep pocket inspection boxes" inside an Internet network can track consumer visits and deliver precise data to anyone eager to sell products or influence opinion and taste.

Perhaps the most significant online breakthrough is the use of "virtual" manufacturing, sometimes described as nanotechnology. Products can now be produced in a virtual world without real mock-ups or materially based forms. From airplanes and cars to buildings and homes, a nonmaterial world of products can be constructed; in fact, it is being constructed, as Boeing's 787 aircraft indicates.

In a world where information and ideas count more than material resources, the gap between rich and poor will diminish in time. In fact, companies that relied on a stable of scientists or so-called experts will now be challenged by the globalization of the Internet. If a question is posted thousands of people across the globe will be able to address it in real time. Knowledge will be democratized as the aggregate views of mankind tackle issues from desertification to agricultural yield.

That technology is changing our lives is apparent as the cell phone, iPods, and HDTV demonstrate. I would be remiss, however, if I mention only the benefits without considering the drawbacks.

A generation that relies on the Internet for research seeks specific answers to specific questions. The large universal, deeply philosophic matters are overlooked. Moreover, if intellectual property is made available without charge-the manifest form of Internet transactions-what is the incentive for scholarship?

Second, the value of the Internet is anyone can use it (this is the height of egalitarianism), but the major flaw is anyone can use it. This technology can be employed to spread knowledge and to spread rumor, to elevate the human experience and to degrade it. The fact that a false rumor can circulate the globe in seconds should give us pause.

Third, by monitoring individual preferences through advanced targeting devices, privacy can be jeopardized. Do I want advertisers to know my desires? Do I want all the information about myself collected and made readily available to a source I do not know?

As Descartes[2] noted when he discussed "the ghost in the machine," technology offers wonders that can influence living, but it is accompanied by a cost. It is one thing to see a world that is flat with opportunity universalized, but it is not far-fetched to envision a Brave New World as well. The choice is clearly ours...or is it? Technology seemingly has momentum of its own. Once in motion, it is hard to stop. Hence, it is wise to think through the pros and cons of new technology and never lose sight of the law of unintended consequences.

Suppose, just suppose, you desire anonymity, a faceless existence in the digital age. You want to get lost in your own thoughts, far from the madding crowd, a stranger in a distant land. Well, it is now close to impossible.

The electronic world closes in on you narrowing the boundaries of privacy. Soon GPS sensors will be in your car identifying how far you have driven and where you are located. Millions of Americans are on Facebook engaged in advertisements for themselves.

Almost every day a new community of electronic exchanges emerges asking you to chronicle your every move. In the last two days alone I have been admonished three times by well-wishers who want to know why I'm not "twittering." I don't tweet.

It strikes me as so strange that everyone-almost everyone-is holding a public mirror that says, look at me. These digital communities admittedly have a leveling effect because well-known and not-so-well-known people participate. Do I really want to know every aspect of their private lives? Why would I want to share my daily activities with people I scarcely know?

The demand for these connections, increases exponentially each week. People have asked me to join Plaxo, LinkedIn, and several other communities. I always join because I don't want to offend a presumptive friend, but I really don't use the sites. I'm not that interested in Harry's new apartment or Mary's new boyfriend.

What does this all mean? My guess is digital communication makes it easier and seemingly more desirable to reveal yourself than, say, telephone conversation. Moreover, you can actually see those with whom you communicate. As I see it, that's something of a problem because I would prefer to rely on my imagination than a computer screen. Then again, I'm hopelessly old fashioned.

All of these digital communication techniques are a part of a modernity that insists privacy is outdated. This isn't exactly Big Brother, but it could be if manipulated by the wrong people. At the moment, it is simply frivolous, a kind of jejune exercise.

Facebook is simply the photogravure with citations. "Look at me; I'm cute and I have many friends who appreciate my winning personality." Should I care? For me these communities do have a vital purpose. They help with a job search. Recommendations are placed online in little boxes and edited by the job searcher. Does it actually lead to employment? I haven't the foggiest idea nor do I have any way of finding out.

What I do know is that much of what appears offends me. There is so much I do not want to read or see. Intimate details in a life I do not know

The Transformational Decade   83

are strangely voyeuristic. There was a time when these details weren't anyone's business and it was tasteless to discuss them.

That, of course, is the rub: Taste is a casualty of this openness. The prevailing sentiment is to let it all hang out. Some teens and I expect adults as well send naked photos and pictures of those in a compromising position, pictures that might not be sent in another medium.

McLuhan is right, the medium is the message. People conduct themselves differently in digital communication. It explains why anonymity is a dying institution. Your business is becoming everyone's business. Because the public is increasingly nosy this activity can be monetized into advertising dollars.

I see it as a form of "freak show" where you pay admission and can see sights only your imagination can conjure. The more you watch, the more intoxicating it becomes until one lives a life on BlackBerry. Personality sites hound you: Why aren't you tweeting? I'm castigated by indignant acquaintances who ask why I remain an "elitist" unwilling to join the multitudes of electronic addicts.

I'm clearly hoping for a return to simpler days that will probably never come. Nonetheless, I remain somewhat firm in my conviction that anonymity is good. Yes, I will not tweet. As I've noted, there are many sound reasons for my reluctance, but aside from voyeurism is the absurdity of the commentary itself.

America is going through a revolution in "dumbing down." There is scarcely an idiocy that doesn't get public attention. Paris Hilton puts her marginal I.Q. on display for public delectation. Anna Nicole Smith displays her physical endowments and mental deficiency for television audiences who expect her to express incoherent commentary.

Of course, idiocy is not new. Even public idiocy had its place, as the Three Stooges demonstrate. The thing that sets this current dumbness craze apart from the past is that it is now a regular feature of television viewing. Being dumb is a television staple.

Jay Leno invites idiots to offer statements on current events. When asked about arms control treaties, these dumb and dumber candidates say things such as "people should be restrained from swinging their arms in public." Leno recently asked two people to travel to an unknown destination. When they arrived in Seattle, they were asked to describe where they might be. Upon seeing the Needle from the World's Fair, they said "this is a place where rockets are launched."

After being told they were in Washington, the young lady wanted to know where the Capitol was located. Her companion seemed mystified about the experience. He maintained that the state was named Washington because this is "where George cut down the apple tree." When told Washington cut down a cherry tree, he wanted to know if that tree was also cut down in Washington.

There was simply no way to extricate these brainless characters from their mental fog. Every answer led to new excursions in silliness. These dupes mercifully didn't have any idea they were the butt of Leno's routine. My guess is they were probably happy to be on television. One might call it ten minutes of infamy.

Smart folks clearly occasionally appear on *Jeopardy* and infrequently some commentator makes an illuminating point on cable TV, but these examples are increasingly the exception. It might well be asked why this should be the case. Whatever happened to the "Quiz Kids" who in my youth were widely admired? When did dumb become chic?

As I see it radical egalitarianism fostered the view that every opinion has validity. Even to suggest that some opinions are stupid is to be charged with elitism, a searing condemnation. Opinions are not dumb; they are simply different. In fact, the word *dumb* has entered a condition of desuetude.

It is also true that in an affluent society there is room for everything, even idiocy. Leno's useful dupes now populate university campuses mouthing clichés about freedom in Third World governments that would never countenance any form of disagreement.

From scientists at MIT who speak an arcane language of quarks to Valley Girls who speak in the shorthand of breathless fools, evidence for degradation as well as elevation exist. America is a nation of every paradox the mind can conjure. At one time, if you called information in New York you dialed "uptight" and in Los Angeles you dialed "popcorn."

It is also true, however, that dumb and dumber are gaining ground; one might even say dumb is chic. There were always eggheads and nerds who were the source of ridicule. At the same time, idiocy was generally not admired. One surely wasn't given television time for being dumb; one was given a program for acting dumb.

Reality TV and the excesses of mass entertainment have converted semi-serious programming into nonsense. The more nonsensical the better. Rather than act, the actors are obliged to be themselves. If you can find a candidate whose brain has been fried by drugs (pace: Ozzy Osbourne) put a camera and mike in his face and have him rant.

It is hard to know exactly when this trend began, but I'm confident we are now in its full efflorescence. Jay Leno has his own version of the Quiz Kids. Three contestants see who can offer the most stupid answers for simple questions. The winner, of course, is the one with the fewest correct responses.

Even the Miss America contest has gone down this path. Finalists are asked questions about history and current affairs. They clearly strive to get the right answers and are disappointed when they are wrong; yet remarkably this supposedly intelligent group invariably knows very little. Is this designed to make viewers who know very little feel better about themselves?

Spoiled kids of the Paris Hilton variety who have money to burn know Versace, but not Descartes. "Oh, isn't that a dessert?" This rich society can live with them, I guess. Whether we prosper with them is another question. These moral vacuums spread chaos wherever they go, albeit unbeknownst to them. Life is a bowl of cherries for Paris, but ask the folks in Altus, Arkansas (where her program "The Simple Life" was made) what they think and the locals will tell you this airhead left a literal and figurative mess behind her.

As I see it, dumb and dumber TV is leaving a mess behind as well. If the brain needs exercise to avoid atrophying, this latest television fare is on its way to producing a generation of mental paralytics. How I yearn for the days of *The Answer Man*.

Just as one needs to pass a driver's test to get a license, I propose that people who appear on TV should pass a knowledge test. I realize some will describe this proposal as hopelessly elitist, but it sure beats mindless and stupid television programming-at least that's one man's opinion.

The Intercollegiate Studies Institute (ISI)[3] recently completed a study on American civic literacy that should serve as a wake-up call for every educator in the country. Since America's founding, leaders have argued that our nation cannot be free and ignorant at the same time. If this study can be relied on, however, that is precisely the predicament in which we find ourselves.

Charles Eliot, former president at Harvard, once said, "The reason there is so much intelligence at this college is freshmen bring so much in and seniors take so little out." Mr. Eliot's glib assertion was actually prescient.

According to the study, "There is a trivial difference between college seniors and their freshmen counterparts regarding knowledge of America's heritage." Overall, college seniors failed the civic literacy exam. More than half could not identify the century when the first American colony was established in Jamestown. A majority did not recognize Yorktown as the battle that brought the American Revolution to an end.

In addition, more than half of the college seniors did not know the Bill of Rights prohibits the establishment of an official religion and, remarkably, nearly half did not know that *The Federalist Papers* were written in support of the Constitution's ratification.

What is going on here? The most highly educated generation, if one is reliant on college attendance, seems to know very little and, more significantly, does not learn very much while in the Academy. Thorstein Veblen's comment that students "are trained in incapacity" takes on new and poignant meaning.

Some might argue that these results apply to marginal colleges and universities, but they would be wrong. An Ivy League education contributes nothing to a student's civic knowledge. Of the fifty schools in the survey, including Brown and Yale, sixteen showed "negative learning." To wit: The seniors in these colleges scored lower than freshmen, "suggesting that they will graduate with even less civic knowledge than what little they had as freshmen."

It is self-evident that colleges that require a course in American history and institutions outperform those schools that do not. In fact, civic learning appears to be related to a traditional core curriculum. A lesser known college like Calvin College achieved a high ranking partly because its students took an average of 1.5 philosophy courses compared with 0.8 philosophy courses taken by seniors at Yale, Berkley, and Johns Hopkins.

The study similarly suggests that civic learning is related to active citizenship. Students with knowledge of American history tend to be more engaged in voting, community service, and political campaigns. Family discussion clearly helps to compensate for deficiencies at colleges, but whether it can compensate fully for curriculum omissions is unclear.

It should be obvious-but often isn't-that our democratic republic needs to be nourished by citizens well versed in our traditions and unique institutions. As this extraordinary study reveals, America's colleges and universities are unfortunately failing in this mission, leaving many college seniors bereft of the fundamental knowledge good citizenship demands.

Where will this ignorance of American life lead? It is hard to predict; however, on one matter there cannot be any doubt: A people unfamiliar with their traditions will not be ardent about defending them. America needs citizens well versed in how exceptional this nation is. If our colleges cannot produce these people, our enemies will know how to exploit this vulnerability. Some might contend that is already happening. That is why we should all be indebted to ISI for this study and why it is time for our colleges and universities to address this fundamental need.

Perhaps some are getting the message.

In the heart of the heartland in Sioux City, Iowa, a "pitchfork mentality" emerged. In a town that has stockyards and a meatpacking company that yields what locals call "aroma alley," the Republican base, which was in retreat since the presidential election, became energized with the Democratic majority growing angry at its own leaders.

Two issues emerged as critical: a government plan to prevent the deductibility of state taxes on the federal tax form and a state Supreme Court decision to mandate homosexual marriages.

If subject to a vote these proposals would have lost 85-15 percent according to recent polls, yet the state court was seemingly oblivious to public sentiment and intent on making the law rather than interpreting it. The Democratic majority in the legislature anticipated a revenue windfall if the tax proposal passes, a windfall it cannot resist.

These two issues were the front burner matters in a state that voted for Barack Obama in the presidential election, but this support for the president evaporated quickly. In Sioux City even the Democrats at a recent rally contended, "he is moving too fast and too far." Iowans believed America was sliding into a command economy that imperils freedom. Despite the claims by hard-core leftists like Janeane Garafalo that these cross-country tea parties are nothing more than discontent with the president's race, I couldn't find a scintilla of evidence to support this claim.

The concern was real and deeply felt, uniting most Republicans and many Democrats. These are rumblings in the heartland that President

Obama should heed, although that doesn't appear to be the case. Iowa farmers don't know John Maynard Keynes, but they do know a power grab when they see one. Fiercely individualistic Iowans are resistant to a Washington bureaucracy that wants to tell them how to live and work. Priming the pump is seemingly acceptable as a method for kicking the economy into gear until the decisions affect personal behavior.

I don't know if Americans are yet ready for a second American Revolution as some bloggers are suggesting, but I do know that anger is building that may be unprecedented in a state conservative in outlook and disposition. The "I'm angry and won't take it any more" refrain at rallies is often bipartisan with some Democrats saying if we only knew "this is the change we've been waiting for," they might have kept on waiting.

The Iowa caucus admittedly launched the Obama campaign for president, about which some Iowans are quite proud. Many state Democrats argue it is still too early to assess the president's performance. That may be true, but the policy directions established with the Stimulus Bill, the Appropriations Bill, and the budget proposal indicate an enormous transfer of capital from the private to the public sector and an accompanying transfer of power as well. This change cannot be overlooked even for those inclined to support the president.

It is possible that if there is an uptick in the economy, the public mood may change; however, it will soon be obvious blame cannot be leveled against former President Bush for the problems Obama inherited. Both the proposals and the state of the economy will soon belong to President Obama and his team; therefore excuses and rationalizations are not likely to fly.

As I see it, the tea parties are a genuine *cri de coeur*. They arise as a plaintive eruption from the grass roots. Where this will lead is anyone's guess because these events are dispersed across the country. At the moment, no one to my knowledge has attempted to translate the evident frustration into a political movement, but that could happen.

President Obama has chosen either to ignore or dismiss these actions. That is a major error. He would be far wiser to address the concerns directly. The longer the anger festers, the more it becomes an impediment to his political fortunes. These tea parties may augur a change as formidable as the one America once experienced in Boston Harbor.

From what source do we find inspiration?

With daily reports of financial corruption roiling Wall Street markets, with terrorism hanging as a dark cloud over America, with the nation increasingly rights-obsessed, atomistic, intellectually indolent, and culturally decadent, it would appear to be time for a transformative political statement that is uplifting and simultaneously offers guidance for the future.

As I see it, Teddy Roosevelt's[4] claim at the outbreak of World War I is a statement for our time, the intellectual equivalent of "back-to-the-future." He noted, "the things that will destroy America are prosperity-at-any-price, peace-at-any-price, safety-first instead of duty-first, the love of soft living and the get-rich-quick theory of life..." Here are words startlingly prescient as the high-octane, high-living 1990s morphed into economic scandal and the evisceration of financial assets in the present.

Roosevelt reminded America that what counts "in the great battle of life" is not wealth, beauty, or even intelligence, but character and, above all in his cosmology, "courage, perseverance, and self-reliance."

T.R. might well have been criticized for his ardent acceptance of social Darwinism, but he knew how to inspire his fellow Americans and he knew as well what was at the very core of this exceptional nation.

Consider his claims. He excoriated "prosperity at any price." We now know from Enron to Adelphia that some corporate leaders were willing to exaggerate earnings in order to bolster their net worth. Deception was built into their *Weltanschauung*, deception born out of culture that maintained the end justifies the means with wealth as the singular end.

We now know from many examples in the 1990s that excusing terrorist acts or refusing to confront them only emboldens the Al-Qaedas of the world. Rather than bring peace, appeasement hastens the onset of war, the presumptive lesson of the Munich Accord in the 1930s.

We now know that being risk averse-counting only on fear avoidance-does not build character or develop manliness. Duty to the family and the nation emerge from calculated risks that promote a welfare greater than the artificial cultivation of self-esteem.

We now know that "soft living" results in degeneracy, an unwillingness to consider anything but sensate pleasures as the spirit desiccates and the soul is made barren. Constant television viewing is the quintessential contemporary acceptance of the soft and ill-considered life.

As political parties retreat from large ambitions and as they shamelessly pander to narrow constituencies and base motives, it is useful to recall that political rhetoric once appealed to the best in the human imagination. It isn't that men once had chests and now they possess only sensitivity; rather, it is the appeal to a higher calling that is missing.

Perhaps in the aftermath of 9/11 Americans will awaken from a fascination with the ephemeral, but this position assumes that the nation can overcome decades of debauchery and self-indulgence. It assumes as well that in the absence of a political vision people will spontaneously recognize the need for truly rewarding pursuits.

T.R. may not be a man for all ages, yet in his persona he offered an image for young people to pursue. He gave America a spiritual dimension sorely lacking at the moment. He had a chest.

It seems to me a person in either party who can recapture this spirit would be elected president. This is probably what pundits mean when they refer to the "vision thing."

"National greatness conservatives" are wise to rely on T.R. as a mentor, but this can only go so far. They must wrap Roosevelt's inspirational message with the idioms of the moment; uniting the past to the present. Young people want to hear that the derision of an inevitable death can be overcome by the soul's flowering in special deeds and in the display of personal and national character.

Chapter 6
The End of Bipartisanship

Since the fall of Communism, progressives have been unembarrassed by the failure of their ideal and are instead emboldened to press for even greater growth of government. The conservative opposition caved in rapidly as the Bush administration tried to accommodate progressive ideas in the name of compassion. Conservatism remains in disarray, though the Tea Party movement is becoming a possible alternative.

In a *New York Times* article[1] Geoffrey Nunberg, a Stanford linguist, argued that bias in the media has undergone great change in the last fifty years so that now it is "a synonym for partiality or partisanship."

He went on to note that conservatives complain about bias yet see "objectivity not as an ideal to strive for but as a dangerous delusion." "Media bias" became a phrase that blurs "the distinction between thoughts and deeds," a condition that enables critics to argue that balance is "better served by openly partisan commentary than by traditional 'objective' reporting."

Dr. Nunberg maintains that "if objectivity is an illusion, we are free to disbelieve any report we find inconvenient or uncongenial on the grounds that it is colored by a hidden agenda." Alas, that is increasingly the case.

Far be it for me to speak for conservatives, or media critics for that matter, but in several essential ways I believe Dr. Nunberg missed the point.

There is a difference between reports and editorials, a distinction often overlooked at the *New York Times*, among other publications. Reports should strive for facts. It was once the case, before the "new journalism," that reporters had to cover stories without the use of adjectives. A condition in which reports can be confused with editorial opinion is a major part of the problem in the current state of journalism.

Second, most people don't have a problem with partisan commentary when it is labeled properly. It is instructive that Dr. Nunberg noted Rush Limbaugh expresses conservative opinion and Michael Moore "very liberal" opinion. If there were truth in labeling Moore should be defined as a radical or an extremist, a characterization he often adopts for himself.

During the riots that emerged after the Rodney King incident, an ABC newsman interviewed gang members who pummeled innocent white drivers in their south central Los Angeles neighborhood. He referred to these thugs as "community leaders." The irony is they called themselves "gang members."

Last, whether journalistic reports are factual or there is reliance on opinion, all commentary should lead ultimately to the search for truth, recognizing that truth is often elusive. Journalism is not merely a tower of Babel with all opinion equally valid. Nor is it a search for dry, incontrovertible facts. Bias invariably insinuates itself into reports, but it would help the reader and the viewer if that bias were recognized.

I suspect the public is skeptical of news reporting because it realizes that while bias exists, many newscasters refuse to acknowledge it. There is the additional confusion over degrees of bias. Although it may be impossible to expunge, there is a difference between a report that tries to be fair and an opinion that makes no effort to do so. It is somewhat like saying because bacteria cannot be completely removed from a hospital operating room, it is comparable to an open sewer. Efforts at fair-minded reports should be recognized as different from opinions and editors would be wise to differentiate the front page of newspapers from the op. ed page.

Dr. Nunberg is surely correct in asserting that bias exists, yet some commentators are more biased than others. As I see it, journalists should be interested in pursuing the truth. If that isn't the case, journalists should at least be defined accurately. It would help if the public knew, before the commentary began whether the spokesman is a liberal, conservative, or radical. This would be a service to the public, and it might even have some influence on written and spoken statements.

Journalists may have a platform for commentary, but in a sense so does everyone else. If one goes to a barber, you expect to pay for a haircut, not political commentary. One may get the latter, but only if you are satisfied with the former. Of course, you can always tell your barber just to "zip it."

In this era everyone has a political opinion which they don't have any qualms about sharing with strangers. My *former* dentist once told me- after I said "have a good day"-that "it would be a good day if George Bush loses the election." Needless to say, she is entitled to her political view, but I didn't go to see her for political guidance.

At a concert in a Broadway theater Mandy Potemkin proceeded to deliver a political diatribe against the Bush administration. I'm sure most of those in the audience didn't pay $65 to hear a political speech, but they got one nonetheless.

In the much acclaimed play "Spelling Bee" there is snide commentary about Karl Rove that has nothing to do with the storyline; it is merely the playwright's way of saying, "I don't like this administration."

Hollywood, of course, is notorious for political innuendo. Whenever there is some buffoon on screen, the protagonist is likely to say, "Oh, he must be a Republican." (Pace: the "Wedding Crashers")

Now if I spend ten bucks for a comedy about two guys who crash weddings in order to pick up women, I don't want unnecessary political commentary. In Hollywood productions, you can be sure you'll get it.

It is different, of course, if you go to hear a performer engage in a political riff, whether it's Jackie Mason or Mort Sahl. One goes to see these comedians with the expectation politics will be inserted into the routine.

The problem I have is with gratuitous politics, those unexpected moments when the bass player insists on telling an audience, "Bush is a creep," or worse. Why would musicians think anyone is interested in their political views?

As a proponent of First Amendment freedom I am certainly not advocating stifling debate or, for that matter, the expression of silly comments; however, I do find it objectionable to pay a lot of money for entertainment that gratuitously offers something other than what's been advertised.

That said, I have a modest suggestion. Just as films have ratings on sexual content and excessive violence, it might be appropriate to have political ratings (e.g., although this film is about the mating habits of gorillas, the director believes it is appropriate to engage in political commentary). As the consumer I should know what I'm going to see along with the advertised content.

This matter is made particularly egregious because the patron of the arts is now obliged to listen to political propaganda in order to hear a performer sing or watch two guys make fools of themselves on screen.

Some might contend that this is no more than *caveat emptor*. I would contend there should be truth in advertising. If a performer insists on propagandizing, I should know about it. Give me the performer's "political rating" before I purchase a ticket.

In the end, those who want to hear Bush or Clinton bashing will decide whether to attend a concert, recital, play, or film. At the very least, the ticket buyer should know what is coming.

On some level this is quite strange. There was a time, not so long ago, when polite conversation and performances excluded sex, gossip, and politics. Now all bets are off. Everything is fair play, most especially one's political views.

Should I really care if Mick Jagger hates neo-cons? My suspicion is Mick Jagger can't find Baghdad on a map of the globe. If someone buys a ticket to a Rolling Stones concert, I would guess the music and spectacle is what one wants to hear and see.

I could be wrong, but I think the public might very well be interested in my novel rating system. Perhaps "PP" for political propaganda can be inserted next to "R" or "PG." For this patron of the arts, it would be a refreshing development.

It is apparent, or should I say should be apparent, that Hollywood would like to refashion the nation in its own image.

At a 2004 concert in Los Angeles Barbra Streisand sang her signature song, "People," with new lyrics she prepared. In her version she describes Secretary of Defense Donald Rumsfeld "the spookiest person in the world" and Secretary of State Colin Powell as "neither fish nor fowl." She ends this revised version of the song with a flourish: "They're lying... while the globe is frying. And the fishes are dying ... in the world."

Needless to say, Ms. Streisand is entitled to her views and she certainly has the right to espouse them publicly. It is also clear that she is an exemplar of Hollywood attitudes and that filmdom's heroes express a mantra that is distinctly homogenous.

This is a view that includes: a distaste for the Bush administration, a relentless devotion to secular trends, a belief in sexual freedom bordering on license, a commitment to expression of any kind, and an antipathy to American corporations.

Let me cite further examples. John Mellencamp, in a song entitled "Texas Bandito," called President Bush "another cheap thug who sacrifices our young." Not to be outdone, Chevy Chase said the president is "as bright as an egg timer." In an episode of *Law and Order* detective Ed Green refers to President Bush as "the dude who lied to us." Of course one can easily find hundreds of other examples from late night talk show hosts to self-appointed political critics like Tim Robbins or Sean Penn.

In one episode of *Curb Your Enthusiasm*, the star Larry David is about to commit adultery when he sees a framed portrait of President Bush on his lover's night table. That destroys the moment. In Hollywood, anti-Bush sentiment even trumps sex.

The reflexive left wing agenda also manifests itself in allegiance to unadulterated environmentalism. *The Day After Tomorrow* is a film that shows the cataclysmic climate effect when the Kyoto Accord isn't honored. Quasi-Marxism raises its Hollywood head in many ways. In the remake of *The Manchurian Candidate* director Jonathan Demme alters the original communist menace into an avaricious multinational corporation with the corporate villain made into a character reminiscent of former Vice President Cheney.

America is invariably evil and religious devotees are fanatics except, of course, for those who embrace Kabala, a mystical Jewish faith. Anyone who believes restriction on expression of any kind, most especially pornography, is considered repressed and a prude-Hollywood's version of a scathing criticism.

As in *Wedding Crashers*, it is instructive that whenever film characters are "uptight," wealthy, or privileged, they are described dismissively as Republicans, notwithstanding the fact that Democrats populate more of the top 1 percent of income earners than Republicans, and that Hollywood has a disproportionate share of the truly wealthy. This irony, of course, is lost on most film moguls.

In the postmodern world Hollywood has come to embody, politics is more important than facts. Most directors and actors make no bones about their political views. Many characterize their craft as an attempt to subvert, disrupt, and destroy patriarchal, imperialist, racist consciousness, as they understand these conditions. In the process they have created an orthodoxy of their own, as strict and obsessive as the orthodoxy they oppose.

If Hollywood of the past, circa pre-1960, was informed by bourgeois cultural values, the Hollywood of today rejects them completely. When presidential candidate John Kerry made reference to Hollywood as the soul of America, he either didn't watch contemporary films or he was pandering to those who offer him support.

Script writers obviously need their villains. If the bad guys in the past were criminals, abusers, dissimulators, and low-lifes, the bad guys of contemporary film are Republicans, corporate leaders, religious figures, and "virtuecrats."

Even documentaries have fallen into the ideological trap of postmodern theory. Documentaries once described a slice of life, an attempt at authentic representation. With *Fahrenheit 9/11* truth took a back seat to political diatribes. It is no longer what happened, but what could have happened or what the director thinks happened.

No one of good will and common sense questions the right of Hollywood stars to speak out, or even to insert their political message into their films. Audiences are free to attend or reject Hollywood's cultural fare. Just as these stars are free to express themselves, critics should be free to explain Hollywood's effort at proselytizing and the orthodoxy that now prevails in the world of film.

Actor Tim Robbins stated that "a chill wind is blowing" across this land. What he was getting at is his belief that the First Amendment is a casualty of the war with Iraq. This belief was manifest after Dale Petroskey, president of the baseball Hall of Fame, canceled a scheduled appearance by Robbins to celebrate the *Bull Durham* film in which Tim Robbins appeared.

According to Robbins this cancellation violated his right to speak out against the war in Iraq. Despite a public apology by Mr. Petroskey, Robbins has escalated his rhetoric into a *cause celebre*, a position he clearly covets.

Despite my distaste for Robbins' opinions and the ignorance he normally displays, he has a point. The First Amendment does allow people to make fools of themselves. It is precisely unpopular opinion-even silly opinion-that is protected.

The government should not be in a position to suppress dissent unless it can be demonstrated that dissent takes the form of conspiracy or sedition and is a threat to the welfare of the nation, what the Supreme Court called "a clear and present danger."

It should also be noted that not every opinion need be expressed. Private groups may deny someone a platform. That, too, is a right. It certainly can be argued that the Hall of Fame is a private organization in a position to decide who will receive invitations to speak.

The only reason why I believe Robbins has a point is that the Hall of Fame is a quasi-public institution. Its standing as a national center puts it in a unique position. Petroskey is technically right in suggesting he can deny anyone the right to speak there, but in my opinion he made a mistake in judgment.

It would have been far better to invite Robbins to speak and invite another Hollywood actor, say Tom Selleck who appeared in a film about baseball and who most probably would support the administration's position on the war, to speak as well.

As I see it, Robbins should be put in a position where he is obliged to defend his views. If Hollywood actors choose to employ their celebrity status for positions on public policy, they should be held accountable. The puerile recitation of Robbins' views deserves public opprobrium. He should be held accountable for his stand. If his defense is predicated on a foundation of sand, he should be allowed to sink in his own self-made swamp.

I have little confidence in Sheen, Sarandon, Streisand, et al.-the Hollywood left that claims to speak for "the people." In fact, it would be far better for the polity if they kept their mouths shut and stuck to acting. On the other hand, free speech doesn't offer a warrant on what should be said. People can say absurd things. The rest of us, however, have an obligation to call them to account.

Because Martin Sheen is an actor who plays the president on the *West Wing* does not qualify him as a spokesman on public policy issues. In fact, I have far more confidence in the positions of my local dry cleaner than Mr. Sheen.

Sheen surely does not speak for me, nor does Tim Robbins; however, the unique dimension of American life is that unpopular, even foolish opinion, cannot be quashed by government action unless it poses a threat to public safety.

Mr. Robbins is only a threat to himself. There is an old Chinese proverb that Robbins should take to heart. *If you don't know very much, say very little. If not, people who thought you might be a fool are likely to be convinced of it.*

When Chris Matthews of *Hardball* indicated that it was "our job" to get Obama elected and then to make him look good, a new chapter in national journalism emerged. By any stretch of the imagination this was cheerleading, not journalism. In the several months since Barack Obama acceded to the presidency, Americans witnessed the equivalent of the Adoration of the Magi.

This schoolgirl crush knows no bounds. Obama's reliance on the teleprompter is explained as a desire to assert a tightly knit and well-thought-through message. One might just as well argue the president cannot deliver a message extemporaneously.

His mistakes are viewed as timing issues. During a G-20 speech in London the president attempted to equate the language in the Declaration of Independence with sloganeering during the French Revolution- a dubious analogy to begin with. After saying "liberté," he stopped and seemingly lost his way. This awkward pregnant pause was thwarted when his eyes found the teleprompter and the words "égalité and fraternité." Members of the press, however, described this as a pause for "emphasis."

Even the president's odd apology to the assembled nations, which legitimized anti-American sentiment ("the U.S. was sorry for wrecking transatlantic relations"), was greeted as the beginning of a healthy relationship with our allies.

The *New York Times*, caught in the Messiah syndrome, rationalizes every word from the president's lips as thoughtful and articulate. Moreover, as A.A. Gill noted (4/5/09) when the president stepped up to 10 Downing Street, he shook the hand of a police officer standing guard and as a consequence, "showed the British how to be classlessy classy." Maureen Dowd argued that Barack Obama "grew up learning how to slip in and out of different worlds-black and white, foreign and American, rich and poor." He "knows how to manipulate." As opposed to George W. Bush who was "manipulated."

As ever, Bush is the handy stooge, the polar opposite of Obama. For the *Times'* columnists Bush is the exemplar of everything that went wrong, the cowboy rough around the edges. Suppose, for the sake of argument, that Bush shook the hand of the bobby standing guard at the prime minister's residence. My guess is the headline would have read "the unclassy Bush does it again and violates diplomatic protocol."

The press surely should point out positive things a president does, but journalism and cheerleading aren't compatible. The president has his public relations hacks who attempt to put a positive spin on everything he says and does. He doesn't need a sycophantic press corps. In fact, an honest portrayal of presidential action is what the country requires.

The American public is instead getting a consistently worshipful tone. Writing in the *Washington Post*, Tom Shales[2] described a presidential press conference in the following way: "Most of the facets of President Obama's personality that have made him intensely popular were on display last night during his second prime-time news conference, and so he emerged from it still every inch 'President Wonderful,' as it were, untouched and intact."

Because of this cupidity, policies are overlooked, policies that are changing the face of America. What we have in its place is a personality cult with image replacing substance and press bias substituting for reportage. If this honeymoon continues unabated Americans may witness the most formidable policy shifts in the history of this nation without journalistic accounting.

The press love affair with Obama may make him look good, but whether this is a healthy state of affairs for the nation remains questionable. I prefer to pray for the Messiah rather than pray to the Messiah the press corps has invented.

Defining who our candidates are and what they stand for is a complicated business, but it is often amusing to see how candidates define themselves.

Senator Hillary Clinton, addressing supporters at a fundraiser in Quogue, said, "I deplore the radical left and the extremists on the religious right. I am in the 'mainstream'." This is indeed a curious comment from a woman who reflexively defended every position on the left throughout her political peregrination.

There is surely a method to this ploy. Americans don't like extremists, so the senator had veered to the center; but this is not a true center, "a vital center," as Arthur Schlesinger once defined it, but rather a center of her own creation.

Clinton, of course, is not alone. On the day the Senate voted for John Roberts to become the new chief justice of the Supreme Court, Senator Chuck Schumer, who voted against Roberts' approval, said, "I hope he won't impose his ideology on court decisions."

What could this comment possibly mean coming from a man who is deeply committed to an ideology, notwithstanding his denials? If someone believes abortion is a right that must remain untrammeled or that special rights must be conferred to homosexuals, aren't these positions ideological?

It seems to me that the word *ideological* is used as a pejorative when an individual doesn't share your views. Schumer has arrogated to himself the role of ideological litmus tester. When Justice Roberts indicated his first and overarching responsibility is upholding the law, namely the U.S. Constitution, Schumer replied, I would like to see a moderate interpretation of the law. Paraphrasing Justice Scalia, a moderate interpretation of the Constitution is halfway between what the Constitution says and what Schumer might like it to say. That summarizes the senator's view very well, I believe.

It is revealing that Schumer, applying his self-designed liberal test, said, Janice Rogers Brown, a talented pro-life judge, is unqualified for the Supreme Court because of her stance on abortion. She was deemed outside the mainstream. Whose mainstream we are discussing should be patently obvious. Moreover, Schumer seems to have forgotten that no one gave him presidential powers.

When faced with criticism of this kind Senator Schumer relies on *stare decisis*, established precedent, to make his case. He must know, that precedents from "slaves as chattel" to "separate but equal" have been overturned by the Supreme Court. I don't think it is farfetched to consider a Court decision that overturns the *Kelo* case and restores the sanctity of private property.

In this context a conservative is someone who takes the words in the Constitution seriously. As a strict constructionist, the conservative believes the founders knew what they were doing to preserve the republic. Creative interpretation or inventing rights only dilutes state authority and invites the delegitimation of government. Hence, one could make the case that the strict constructionist is in the mainstream. It is the left-leaning Breyers and Ginsbergs who are outside any political mainstream, despite the praise heaped on these judges by the New York senators and the New York press corps.

It is instructive that Ruth Bader Ginsberg, a former ACLU lawyer, appointed to the Court by President Clinton, is considered, in the fevered imagination of Senator Schumer, a moderate. If one agrees with this bizarre assessment, then anyone to the right of Ginsberg-an area in which there is enormous political space-would be considered an extremist.

In the political arena in which language evokes emotion, words such as *moderate, extremist,* and *mainstream* should be put under a microscope of rational analysis. As I see it, these words cease to have any meaning; they have been misshapen by the desire for political advantage.

The next time, a pol says I am in the mainstream but my opponent is not, ask what is meant by mainstream. I think you'll be surprised by the response, or perhaps not, if you are addicted to the mindless recitation of empty clichés that now surround campaigns and political speeches.

The mainstream has clearly made a leftward lurch in many quarters.

Little Red, a Greenwich Village school, with a pure left-wing pedigree recently called on alumni members to engage in a school sponsored "conversation." In order to prompt a response the administration brought attention to two former graduates. One of these grads is Robert Meeropol, class of 1965 and a person described as a "distinguished alumnus."

Mr. Meeropol is described in the invitation as "the founder" of the Rosenberg Fund for children and currently serves as its executive director. "The RFC provides for the educational and emotional needs of both targeted activist youth and children in this country whose parents have been harassed, injured, jailed, lost jobs, or died in the course of their progressive activities." Robert received undergraduate and graduate degrees in anthropology from the University of Michigan and graduated law school in 1985. For the past thirty years he has been a progressive activist, author, and speaker.

What the sanitized language in the invitation conceals is truly extraordinary. Meeropol is the child of Ethel and Julies Rosenberg, two communists executed for espionage. Despite the evidence provided by the Venona papers, Meeropol insists on the innocence of his parents, an understandable reaction, but one based largely on sentiment.

His work on behalf of "targeted activist youth... whose parents have been harassed, injured, jailed, lost jobs, or died in the course of their progressive activities" is ostensibly research that would exonerate his parents. Perhaps the most controversial word in this brief bio is "progressive." Is it progressive to engage in espionage for an avowed enemy of the United States?

Whereas a son's appreciation of his parents-however venal their actions-is easily rationalized, at some point historical realities intrude. Ronald Radosh's history of the Rosenbergs demonstrates beyond any reasonable doubt that they were guilty of crimes against the United States.

This biography was written before the damaging revelations in the Venona papers.

It is noteworthy that Radosh was also a graduate of the Little Red School and for a time embraced its left-wing orthodoxy. Is it merely coincidental that he was not one of the graduates profiled for this alumni reunion?

It is instructive that treasonous activity that took the form of selling secrets about the atom bomb to the Soviet Union should now be called progressive. In the cauldron of Orwellian revision the left can justify any action as long as it has a distinct anti-establishment flavor.

What makes this invitation truly egregious is that a school offers cover for criminal actions. I am aware of the radical claim "no enemies on the left," but I find it hard to believe that criticism of the United States could be transmogrified into reflexive anti-Americanism.

Keep in mind that the Progressive Movement in American history had reformist impulses, but it was deeply nationalistic. Franklin Roosevelt, arguably the most progressive president of the twentieth century, was, despite the allegations of many conservatives, patriotic.

Now "progressive" has been shifted to the outer reaches of left-wing opinion. Because "communist" and "socialist" have been discredited by historical events, "progressive" has been preempted as a catch-all phrase for radical anti-American actions.

The student demonstrators who can be found chanting anti-Bush slogans in Union Square Park on behalf of Ramsey Clark's ANSWER are described as progressives. They blame America: for everything and never concede national achievement.

What makes them progressive is solely an antipathy to American history and national policies. The utopias they believe in from Cuba to Nicaragua reveal their feet of clay in time, but the United States is that old standby, there to be criticized without the benefit of any doubt.

Is it surprising that Meeropol is being profiled at Little Red? No, not really; he comes out of a "proud tradition" that lacks balance, perspective, and honesty. The shadows of the past spread darkness on closed minds and unfortunately many of our schools seal illumination in their classrooms. It is not surprising that what emerges years later is an alumni event jaundiced by the sanitizing of history.

From this darkness emerges an inability to cope with present realities.

Some might call it preemptive surrender; others describe it as appeasement; and still others refer to this condition as falling prey to intimidation. However one describes this phenomenon, it is clear the West is fast becoming overwhelmed by the force of Islam.

Two recent events reinforce this conclusion.

The Media Research Center issued a September 2006 report entitled, "The Media vs. The War on Terror," in which it is pointed out that in general the media leaders are far more interested in exposing tactics that may undermine American civil liberties than in addressing tactics for defeating Islamic radicals.

For example, most of the network coverage of Guantanamo focused on the rights of captured terrorists or allegations that they were mistreated or abused. Network reporters portrayed the inmates as "victims," yet not one report about Guantanamo prisoners included commentary from the genuine victims of 9/11, family members who lost a loved one.

Most network stories cast the NSA's terrorist surveillance program as either legally dubious or illegal. ABC, CBS, and NBC were five times more likely to showcase experts who criticize the NSA's surveillance program than supporters.

At the end of September, Berlin's Deutsche Opera removed the staging of a Mozart opera from its schedule for fear of enraging Muslims, opera house officials said.

Hans Neuenfel's production of "Idomeneo," a 1781 drama set in ancient Crete, was canceled because opera authorities felt it presented an "incalculable security risk." In the staging King Idomeneo presents the lopped-off heads of Poseidon, Jesus, Buddha, and the Prophet Mohammed and displays them on chairs.

Some critics viewed the show as a radical attack on religion, all religions. Music director Kirsten Harms, decided that the staging would be regarded as an insult to Muslims that could result in "danger to the audience or staff" because Islam considers images of the prophet as blasphemous.

Consider the following conditions. Suppose al Jazeera ran programs that described violent tactics employed by Jihadists. Suppose as well that the music director at the Egyptian Opera House chose to promote a production with a pro-American and pro-Israeli theme. So farfetched are these possibilities that they cannot be seriously entertained.

Here, however, is the issue. What is good for the goose is not good for the gander. Intimidation has changed the cultural calculus in the West. As notable, there isn't any sense of reciprocity.

We accept this form of intimidation and appeasement. It is now a cultural given. By contrast, we also expect intolerance from the Islamic world.

It was instructive that Pope Benedict's speech, which quoted from a medieval text that said the teaching of the Prophet Mohammed was "evil and inhuman," sparked Muslim anger. In effect Jihadists were saying that if you say we're intolerant, we will intimidate you with intolerant tactics. (QED)

Where, then, is the West's resolve? Why should we stand by or be complicit in this form of intimidation?

The debate in the future is not over a decision to cancel a performance or whether one has the right to challenge a president. Of course, both should be possible. The real question is do we have what it takes to stand up to the intimidators and assert a defense of our way of life. Recent events give one pause.

With all the attention the world has devoted to the Danish newspaper, *Jylands-Posten's*, cartoons depicting Prophet Mohammed, there are-it seems to me-several conditions surrounding this matter that deserve further elaboration.

First, and perhaps most noteworthy, is the self-censorship many Western observers have imposed on themselves when the riots began. This form of preemptive subservience satisfies Islamists intent on global domination. As many observers have pointed out, freedom of the press has in many instances retreated before selective moral indignation.

The reasons for this response are manifold: fear, sympathy, anti-Western animus, and sensitivity to Muslim beliefs. The sympathizers ignore that without religious mandate they have supinely accepted dominitude, the subservience Muslims demand of nonbelievers.

Although the appropriate stance should be the affirmation of Western principle-namely, freedom of speech-many cower, fearful of offending marauding religious adherents. Instead of meeting speech that may be offensive with counterspeech, Islamists threaten-and in extreme instances engage in murder (e.g. the killing of Theo van Gogh after he made a film depicting the mistreatment of Muslim women).

Even the threats are rationalized. Pat Buchanan noted that these cartoons deserve to be censored and implied that there is justification for the riots. His response is reminiscent of John Le Carré[3], who after learning of a fatwa on Salman Rushdie for the publication of *Satanic Verses*, said, "There is no law in life or nature that says great religion may be insulted with impunity." Le Carré, however, has not been heard when Muslims routinely call Jews monkeys and pigs. What is good for Muslims is apparently not good for what Muslims deplore.

The U.N. high commissioner for human rights, Canadian Justice Louise Arbour[4], responded to a complaint from the Organization of The Islamic Conference by arguing, "I find alarming any behaviors that disregard the belief of others." She proceeded to launch an investigation into "racism" and "disrespect for belief" and asked for an official explanation from the Danish government. It is instructive that the U.N. Human Rights Commission has been conspicuously silent on the vicious portrayal of Jews in the schoolbooks distributed in the Palestinian territory and in many Muslim nations.

Even though the examples cited here do not necessarily constitute a morally flaccid West, they do suggest moral hypocrisy on the part of many on the left who for decades claimed to be seeking liberation from artificially imposed social barriers. Christianity was seen as superstition; taboos as mere synthetic constraints against sexual expression.

Now, however, the left has embraced a position of high dudgeon over the criticism of Islam. Freedom is both sacrificed on the crescent of Islam, and the left has been willing to repudiate its own position in order to be a bedfellow of Islamists.

Feminists, who have fought for women's rights in the United States, have been silent over the abusive treatment of Muslim women. I would have thought acolytes of Betty Freidan would be demonstrating in front of every capital of every Muslim nation. The moral fervor they directed against middle class American men, has been converted into moral osteoporosis, alas moral hypocrisy when it comes to Islam.

Any anti-Western sentiment is apparently worthy of support if it is consistent with a reflexive anti-Western view of the left. The enemy of my enemy is my friend has become a refrain. The libertarians of the left have curiously been willing to embrace fascism of the most reactionary variety.

This red-green nexus is not a Christmas decoration. It is a threat that could undermine basic freedom in the West. The episode over the cartoons is a test. Islamists have fomented riots in an effort to see how the West will respond.

There will be other tests and with each one Islam will demand further observance of dominitude. The question that remains is whether the West will stand up to this challenge with fortitude and coverage. As I see it there isn't any backing down, lest our civilization is put at risk. Here is where politics faces a new and imposing challenge.

There was time not so long ago when Democrats crossed the aisle to support Republican positions in war and vice versa. These were not always instances of gentility and partisanship wasn't ignored; this occasional gesture was a recognition of national welfare that transcended politics.

What one observes with the Democratic party at the moment is an astonishingly anti-American posture that I have not encountered in my lifetime. The impression was created that critics of the Bush administration were more interested in capturing the presidency than in winning the war in Iraq. In fact, if success in the war were attributed to President Bush, they would prefer defeat.

This obviously isn't the position of every Democrat, as Senator Lieberman's stance demonstrates, but it is the Kennedy, Pelosi, Rockefeller, Kerry, and Reid stance. Moreover, two former Democratic presidents, Carter and Clinton, have engaged in what was once taboo for those who sat in the executive office: They have attacked the present administration abroad, in countries already hostile to American interests. Such behavior was always regarded as a "no-no." You might disagree or even criticize a sitting president at home, but to do so outside the confines of the nation and in countries inimical to U.S. interests was simply off-limits.

It seems that the Democratic party has imbibed the Michael Moore approach to politics, which includes equal parts caricature and traitorous commentary. Moore has noted on several occasions that the Iraqi insurgents are the equivalent of the Minutemen and that we must suffer the bloodletting of our young for the misguided policies of our president.

Of course, Moore is not alone. Frank Rich, among others, has engaged in a refrain that the president lied in order to promote the war effort. Despite the evidence that has been marshaled demonstrating a bipartisan concern about weapons of mass destruction prior to Bush's election, the president's detractors cannot let go of this theme.

It is instructive that the word *lie* is employed. Even if you embraced the Frank Rich stance (which I do not), you might say the president was "mistaken," or "misguided" or "misread the signals." Of course, these words are equivocal to offering the president an alibi, a concession the critics are not willing to consider.

The Democratic party position is search and destroy. It is anyone's guess whether this is "get even" time for the Clinton impeachment or the venting of hostility over the 2000 election. It does suggest a parlous political state in which any move that harms the Republican leadership is deemed acceptable.

Bush, by contrast, acted as if Marquis of Queensbury rules applied to this street fight. He was remarkably subdued in the face of continual vitriol heaped upon him. From my perch, I would have preferred greater boldness on his part, a condition I did observe with his Annapolis speech.

Lest I am criticized for challenging criticism, let it be noted that I believe presidents should be criticized when it is appropriate to do so. What I'm getting at is criticism that verges on treason. When polls say that defeat serves us right, they either want to embarrass the administration without regard to the risks involved or they actually think a defeat for the administration is justifiable. That kind of criticism is beyond the pale.

This backbiting may be amusing for news aficionados, but the stakes are high and go well beyond amusement. The Fifth Column in the United States is growing, led by some officials who do not fully appreciate the consequences of their actions. Lives are at stake, regional stability is in the mix, and civilization itself is in the balance.

This is not hyperbole. Al Qaeda is watching and listening. Every anti-American position is music to their ears. For them, it defines a nation that has lost its will and fortitude. The disloyal Americans only embolden the enemies. We've been down this path before, albeit historical lessons have to be relearned. Lives unfortunately will be lost that could be saved and this nation will suffer before the critics learn their lesson.

Speaker of the House Nancy Pelosi insists on a date for the withdrawal of American forces from Iraq. In fact, the Democratic leadership has embraced this position.

The *New York Times* advocated a withdrawal plan and if its campaign to sanitize the Muslim Brotherhood can be seriously entertained, the *Times* seemed to be arguing there isn't that much to worry about in the Muslim world. Tariq Ramadan, a clever spokesman for the Muslim Brotherhood, was featured in the 4/1/09 *Times Magazine* with the claim Islam and democracy are not incompatible.

The Democratic leaders and their acolytes at the *Times* seem to be arguing that stabilizing Iraq cannot be achieved and the United States is suffering from hysteria over the Muslim threat that has resulted in a misguided foreign policy.

It is noteworthy that since "the Surge" conditions in Iraq improved dramatically; however, you wouldn't know that from reading "the paper of record," nor would you get that impression from congressional testimony. As one well-known Iranian journalist noted, "the success of the Democratic party is dependent on the American failure in Iraq." As a consequence, good news in Iraq is bad news for the fortunes of the Democratic party.

If true, this is a sad moment in American history when the lives of servicemen and women are mere pawns for political gain.

Lest my detractors believe this is a diatribe against Democrats, they would be wrong. In my opinion the president has not used his bully pulpit effectively. He should have put the Democratic-led Congress on notice by going directly to the American people and addressing concerns about the war. He should mobilize the Republican party for political warfare in the national media. He should create a War Information Office to make the arguments he doesn't.

What may be at stake in World War IV is not evident to most Americans. The people haven't been asked to sacrifice and they haven't been asked to evaluate the costs and benefits in this war. In fact, many Americans don't realize we are at war, despite tocsin in the Muslim world.

A great divide is emerging in American politics: on one side are Democrats who do not see any value in the Iraq war; on the other side are Republicans, by no means all, who see a great danger in a "cut-and-run" strategy. The two views are mutually incompatible. This stance is complicated by a general perception of the threat imposed by Islam.

Some contend Islam is basically benign, notwithstanding fringe groups that have a militant attitude. Others maintain Islam is inherently violent and has imperial goals that threaten the West. Either Islam is a threat or it isn't. Either the West must protect itself from the onslaught or it shouldn't overreact.

It is clear where Ms. Pelosi stands and where she is taking the Democratic party. It is not clear whether this is in the best interest of the United States. If she is mistaken, there are civilizational consequences that cause even inveterate optimists to shudder.

Democratic leaders are so hostile to President Bush that Zbigniew Brzezinski, a normally reliable analyst of foreign policy, has had sobriety desert him in his new book, *Second Chance*[5], a book in which he engages in a no-holds-barred-attack on the present administration.

The gloves are off and so too is bipartisanship. It seems to me disagreements are useful, but hateful attacks on one another only produce ammunition for the enemy. As I see it, the time has come for Democrats and Republicans to leave politics in the outhouse and consider what is best for the national house in which we all reside.

The Democratic sharks smelled Republican blood in the water. As a consequence, they zeroed in on Karl Rove in order to embarrass the president in what has become a tidal wave of partisanship. It is revealing, however, that these are toothless sharks on a hapless mission.

There is the contention that Karl Rove revealed Valerie Plame's identity as a CIA agent, thereby violating the law (one might call it the Philip Agee precedent) and putting Ms. Plame in a compromised position.

Overlooked in the overheated accusation is that all discussion of Plame's identity was initiated by journalists; Ms. Plame was not an undercover agent at the CIA and, Rove's intentions to the extent they're discernible, were to discredit Plame's husband, Joseph Wilson, who according to British intelligence, lied when he reported that Iraq did not seek nuclear material from Niger.

There you have it, another Washington pettifogging issue. The Democrats, however, are in high dudgeon. Senator Chuck Schumer couldn't contain his sanctimonious utterances by calling for the removal of Rove's security clearance. Senator Joseph Biden called Rove's actions "a national security breach." Senator Hillary Clinton, reflecting on events in the White House, struck a decidedly low note by comparing President Bush with *Mad* magazine's Alfred E. Neuman.

Washington loves farce the way boxing aficionados crave blood. Washington is a "hot house" in which Dems seek to embarrass Reps and vice versa. Democrats are feeling their oats because they believe Bush may be on the losing side of history.

To some degree, the Democrats are in search of the contemporary Watergate. From their perspective Watergate was the nadir of Republican fortunes. On the other side of the aisle, Republicans view the Clinton impeachment as the apogee of their political gamesmanship. As a result each party seeks the embarrassment of the other side in an explosive partisan cauldron.

Today, liberals understand they can tie the administration in knots even if their argument is about a pseudo-event. Does anyone remember how Eisenhower had to bow to press opinion because Sherman Adams, his close associate, accepted the gift of a fancy coat?

Paul Krugman[6], writing in the *New York Times* notes, "There's no question that he (Karl Rove) damaged national security for partisan advantage. If Democrats had done that Republicans would call it treason." In unvarnished form, here are media smear tactics. Rove presumably damaged national security and, if the charge were in the other political direction, it would be treason. These are strong words unmoored from empirical evidence.

This is unfortunately a typical Washington media exercise. Words need not be defined. On either side of the partisan divide people can play fast and loose with the truth. In fact, partisan advantage trumps basic human concerns.

At a time when it is essential that the nation develop a working consensus to deal with a war against terrorism and radical Islam, there is low-intensity conflict in Washington. Democrats have thrown down the gauntlet on this occasion, albeit sensible liberals must realize there isn't much to blow out of proportion. Of course, that won't stop them from trying.

It is ironic that Senator Schumer, to cite one example, is flogging a website "to stop Karl Rove" and, by the way, "build financial resources so we can help our candidates... achieve a Democratic Senate majority." In 1982, however, Schumer worked to defeat the Intelligence Identities Protection Act, which was enacted at President Ronald Reagan's insistence. Schumer now sings a new tune. Could it be related to his position as head of the Democratic Senatorial Campaign Committee? How can any serious person entertain his assertion?

This is the new Washington, the one that inflicts injury by throwing character assassination bombs. In 1968 conservative senators, led by Michigan's Robert Griffin, prevented a vote on LBJ's choice for chief justice of the Supreme Court, Abe Fortas, by hurling fiery invectives against him. Several years ago Robert Bork, arguably the most talented jurist in the nation, was denied a seat on the Supreme Court because of a well-designed liberal media crusade launched against him. Today, Senator Dodd and his well-placed colleagues have thus far prevented John Bolton from securing a position as ambassador to the U.N. on the laughable accusation that he became angry at a former employee.

Washington is electrified through scandal, both the real and the imagined. The real scandal is that during these parlous times the parties should be working together despite their differences. The so-called Rove affair is a mere distraction, a way to make points against an opponent. In the end, this bickering only arouses public cynicism about politicians and enervates the spirit necessary to fight real enemies.

Chapter 7
Ignorance Is Not Bliss

The miseducation of Americans has consequences that run deep in the body politic.

More than a decade ago Ben Wattenberg[1] wrote a book with the marvelous title, *The Good News Is The Bad News Is Wrong*. If that book were republished today I would change the title to *The Bad News Is The Good News Is Ignored*.

It isn't surprising that in the world of media reportage only bad news counts. The problem with this condition is that it feeds a generally one-dimensional view of politics, a misperception of the world that promotes *weltschmerz* and despair.

Most of the reports about Iraq, for example, emphasize sectarian violence, failed policy, and tactical errors. Overlooked, with rare exceptions, is that the "surge" and an emphasis on counterinsurgency have had a profound effect on the war effort. Civilian deaths have fallen 77 percent year over year, while military fatalities have declined by 64 percent.

Needless to say, nirvana has not been achieved, nor is it appropriate to declare victory, but the trend line is clear. Al Qaeda is in retreat. Even many Sunni leaders who had provided sanctuary for Al Qaeda terrorists have turned against them. The *Washington Post* and the BBC finally admitted recently that violence in Iraq is abating, but these stories appeared well into the third stage of the campaign and remained aberrational in media coverage of the war.

Second, it is noteworthy that Democrats have placed a great emphasis on income disparity in the nation. The quasi-Marxist contention is that the rich grow richer and the poor, poorer; however, the evidence provides a somewhat different picture.

The middle class has more disposable wealth than ever before and the lowest quintile has actually improved its annual income. Moreover, the numbers overlook the extraordinary mobility of one group rising and some falling back. Perhaps the most significant finding, is that the percentage of those who are poor had declined slightly and the percentage of those who earn more than $150,000 per annum has increased (controlling for inflation).

Needless to say, this condition may not attract the attention of "two Americas" speechmakers because the reality is much less provocative than assertions of economic exploitation. There surely should be space somewhere in TV land where the nuanced story of class income can be described.

Last, it is often said by the panjandrums of television news that most Americans are dissatisfied with their jobs. Workers are presumably distressed by dreary dead-end positions; however, recent polls tell a different story with more than two thirds arguing that they are satisfied or very satisfied with their present positions.

It should also be noted that most Americans between the ages of 25 and 45 change jobs multiple times indicating that there are several opportunities to find employment satisfaction. In a society that has made the transition from an industrial base to an information-structured economy, those who obtain skills can dictate to the employment market. This may be the first time in history that labor influences management more than the reverse.

These largely undisclosed, or should I say nonpublicized, accounts are part of a consistent media view. In the 1960s it was argued, due in part to Paul Ehrlich's[2] book *The Population Bomb*, that the world's population would double in every subsequent decade. Of course, that hasn't happened, but the recantation hasn't either. It was argued four years ago that several islands in the Pacific would have to be evacuated because the ocean would rise due to global warming, but the devastation of these atolls has not occurred and the media organs responsible for the initial accounts are silent.

The drumbeat of negativism is unrelenting. There may be some good news stories on TV and in newspapers, but it is simply hard to find them. I wonder what kind of effect a steady diet of negative news has on the public. No, I need not wonder; I see it in the mind set of nihilists, who preach despair and the end of the American experiment.

Thomas Jefferson once noted that democracy flourishes when the electorate is informed and flounders when there is a lack of knowledge. This comment is particularly poignant when one considers the general level of ignorance among voters and, as a consequence, the extent to which citizens can be manipulated by elites.

Public policy questions, such as the stem cell debate, are admittedly more complicated than they were in the past, yet the public relies increasingly on short-hand evidence to gain knowledge. The Internet and TV news serve as the primary sources of information.

Political scientist John Ferejohn wrote[3]: "Nothing strikes the student of public opinion and democracy more forcefully than the paucity of information most people possess about politics." Ferejohn is not alone in his assessment. Few scholars would dispute the view that most voters are ignorant of basic political considerations.

In 1964, in the middle of the Cold War, only 38 percent of respondents to a questionnaire were aware that the Soviet Union was not a member of NATO. Almost 70 percent of Americans do not know about the passage of the Medicare prescription drug programs. In addition, 58 percent admit almost no knowledge of the Patriot Act, and 77 percent admit to knowing "little or nothing" about the European Union.

Active misinformation is as significant as the lack thereof. For example, 61 percent of Americans believe that there was a net loss of jobs in 2004. That, by the way, is simply untrue.

Ilya Somin[4] of George Mason University contends that "a large political knowledge underclass of 'know nothings' constitutes from 25 percent to 35 percent of the American public." Some Americans maintain that experience is as valid a guide to politics as knowledge. Although I am somewhat sympathetic to this position, experience is not always a handy guide for policy decisions. Errors about the unemployment rate, for example, are invariably a function of one's employment status.

Even at the college level a lack of basic information is evident. In a recent poll a majority of college students could not identify the decade in which the Civil War was fought; a large majority didn't know whether the American or French revolutions came first and a significant plurality did not know who was responsible for the words, "of the people, by the people, for the people."

It is therefore not surprising that a large number of prospective voters take their cues from opinion leaders (i.e., activists who are intent on promoting a position). Michael Moore, to use one such example, has an axe to grind and a format for reaching many voters. His influence cannot be underestimated. In many instances, however, activist opinions and the average voter's predilections diverge.

Deciphering clever commentary is often difficult, especially if people don't have adequate education. For example, during the presidential debate Senator Kerry said the top 1 percent of income earners received an $87 billion windfall when Bush cut the income tax rate. On its face, this appears unfair; however, if you know that 1 percent of the population pays 34 percent of the personal income taxes and that 49 percent of the population doesn't pay any income tax at all, the Kerry assertions lose their rhetorical power.

The advantage of the American system of voting clearly is that the electorate has the chance to oust those who engage in what it considers a policy failure. First, of course, the voter has to be able to determine a policy failure and, second, he has to be in a position to determine whether another candidate has an adequate remedy.

The ignorant voter often cannot readily discern what is truly in his best interest and whether a policy has failed. Moreover, with ignorant voters the incumbent is often at a disadvantage because his positions have been absorbed into media presentations, whereas the aspiring candidate can postulate on any matter without reference to a readily understood record.

Considering the size and complexity of government, average voters could justifiably contend that making themselves knowledgeable about issues is not a valid trade-off because knowing more doesn't necessarily result in greater influence over the course of government activity. Even professional political scientists often have little more than a superficial knowledge of how Washington actually functions. It is not coincidental that Aristotle, among others, argued that democracy works best when government is limited and the influence of elites is minimized.

What one can do about this issue is a matter leaders should consider, albeit many leaders prefer an ignorant voting bloc; for those of us that take this matter seriously, an electorate that is ignorant of public affairs imperils the representative system and our entire way of life. That is a matter of which we had better not remain ignorant.

Recent polls seem to suggest that a majority of Americans are opposed to the war in Iraq or, at the very least, is suspicious of the administration's motives. It is hardly surprising considering the drumbeat of daily anti-Bush commentary in the press, the Michael Moore documentary, *Fahrenheit 9/11*, and the report from the 9/11 commission.

President George Bush has attempted to explain his position, but it is invariably trumped by a torrent of criticism or is dismissed by cynics as weak rationalization. As daily body counts in Iraq mount, public impatience seems to mount accordingly. Both at home and abroad many people refer to "U.S. arrogance," which usually takes the form of allegations about unilateralism.

Despite all the hysteria and public acrimony, there was never an obvious policy alternative posited by the Democrats. Moreover attempting to calibrate policy to poll results-ala Clinton-would have been a terrible mistake.

On September 30, 1944, Winston Churchill delivered his report on the war to the House of Commons. As a backdrop to his comments, it should be noted that there were appeasers still willing to give Hitler the benefit of the doubt even after Munich; there were Britons tired of the war effort and simply eager for an end, any end, and there were those who believed that if England sued for peace at that time, it might get reasonable terms. In the aggregate these views represented minority opinion, but it was opinion that could not be easily discounted.

Nonetheless, Churchill addressed the House[5] by noting, "Nothing is more dangerous in wartime than to live in the temperamental atmosphere of a Gallup Poll, always feeling one's pulse and taking one's temperature."

This would have been superb advice for President Bush. Notwithstanding all the polls, all the temperature taking, the president simply did what he considered best for the nation, even when its citizens didn't always appreciate his actions.

Polls are a snapshot of public sentiment, but history, the ultimate judge of policy decisions, is a montage. Just as the British resistance to Hitler turned out to be England's "finest hour," it may well be that the U.S. commitment to the eradication of radical Islam and its worldwide terrorist campaign is its finest hour.

It is a cliché to suggest that the president stay the course, yet that is precisely what is needed. Damn the polls; they may change next week or next month in any case. Leadership in a democracy is tricky; a leader cannot be insensitive to those in his constituency. On the other hand, he isn't a leader if he bends to the fickle oscillations of public opinion.

The war in Iraq, Afghanistan, and elsewhere, I should note, is a war for survival. Our national mettle was being tested. Would the president and congressional leaders succumb to a public that had lost the stomach for the fight or would it lead that public into a war for survival?

In a high-income, low-birth rate nation, the answer to that question is not obvious. It is obvious that the nation is being tested by fanatics who believe we do not have the fortitude to fight. It is equally obvious that polls, as an expression of the public mood, are the enemy of sensible policy. Plebiscites don't make for public policy and moods, like the weather, are variable.

Ergo, President Bush should have thought of himself as Churchill-a man committed to the eradication of an evil that would destroy his nation. Any other consideration at the time would be irrelevant.

The 2004 election, however, demonstrated an electorate intensely divided.

For several hours on November 2, the Buckeye state was converted into the "legal eagle" state. Democratic legal teams were ready to swoop into Columbus, the capital, fully prepared to contest the election result.

Although Bush needed Ohio for a victory in the general election, the 136,000 margin of success in the state seemingly assured that result, notwithstanding the examination of provisional votes.

Several television networks, refused to call Ohio a "red state" and despite the president's lead in New Mexico, Nevada, and Wisconsin, the networks would not concede those states to Bush late into the night.

In this case a little history might be useful. In 1960 J.F.K. won the presidency after capturing Texas and Illinois, states where his aggregate margin of victory was about 8000 votes. As historians have duly noted, Chicago Mayor Daley "created votes" and L.B.J., using old Texas techniques, manufactured them.

Recognizing the corruption and the possibility that he may have won the presidency, Richard Nixon, the Republican candidate, conceded, noting at the time that a review of the vote would only tear the nation apart. Whatever Watergate may have done to besmirch his reputation, this gesture was among Nixon's finest hours. He put the welfare of the nation above personal ambition. He did what you would expect a patriot to do. To his credit, Kerry ultimately made a remarkably generous concession speech of his own, albeit much angst could have been avoided if he gave this speech after the Ohio result was announced.

There is yet another factor that should be mentioned even though it is politically incorrect. If the Democrats had wanted to impound all the voting machines in Ohio, Republicans should have demanded the same condition for Newark, NJ, and Philadelphia, PA. According to Republican poll watchers the intimidation against *them* was relentless. Although the claim was made that these poll watchers discourage Democratic voters, they actually discouraged illegal voting procedures. Some reports even suggest that there are districts in Philadelphia where the total vote exceeded the number of registered voters by a sizable margin. "Vote early and vote often" was a cry heard throughout urban America. Perhaps it's time to be clear about who was trying to "steal" the election.

The results may underscore the nation's enduring political divide, but there should be relatively little doubt about which candidate won. In fact, the Democrats cited the popular vote in 2000 arguing that Gore had actually won the election. This time, Bush has command of the popular vote; in fact, he achieved a majority of those voting-something Bill Clinton did not accomplish.

It is fair to argue that the 2004 race deepened partisan divisions in the country. It also seems reasonable, that a concession speech in which unity is stressed could mitigate the tension between the parties.

The sense that much is at stake in this year brought record numbers to the polls. Young people-first-time voters-showed up in large numbers. What lesson, is to be derived from their participation?

It boggles the mind to consider what elections have become. At times I regarded political commentary as America at war with itself. I wondered if the political gap between the parties could ever be bridged and whether civility could be restored. That, of course, is my hope. My hope, however, was not reinforced by the behavior of Democratic stalwarts after the vote came in. If I were asked to comment about the situation, I would say, "Enough already."

In my quest to understand the reaction of losers in that presidential campaign I scoured newspaper editorials across the country. On November 5 in the *San Francisco Chronicle* I struck gold. There in the boldest and most direct terms was the liberal interpretation of what happened on Election Day.

First, there was the inimitable Molly Ivins[6] who wrote, "The Bush administration is going to be wired around the neck of the American people for four more years, long enough for the stench to sicken everybody. It should cure the country of electing Republicans."

Then I read a piece by Sandip Roy[7], an editor at *Pacific News Service*, who wrote: "...on Nov 2, as I saw state after state passing anti-same-sex-marriage amendments, dismantling even the notion of civil unions-the vote was 86 percent to 14 percent in Mississippi-it startled me into realizing how deeply America fears me."

I read with bemusement in London's *Daily Mirror*[8] that 59,054,087 voters in the United States are "dumb."

There you have it: contempt, condescension, and fury. I don't believe this is a common view in this nation or even a view commonly held by Democrats. As one moves to the fringe of the party and the media elites, however, this opinion is not uncommon.

It sometimes appears as if arrogant radicals have arrogated to themselves the right to speak for all Americans. After all, what do those hicks in flyover states know anyway?

Despite Mr. Roy's anger at the rejection of same sex marriage in eleven states where this measure appeared on the ballot, Americans were merely expressing support for a common sense, civilizational concern for marriage as the union between a man and a woman. I don't assume this vote was directed at Mr. Roy or any other homosexual for that matter. It was an expression of concern, a belief that some homosexuals were overreaching in their desire to impose same sex marriage on the nation, thereby changing the institution of marriage itself.

For radicals, the Republicans are imposing moral beliefs on Americans, yet it is instructive that these are the same people who invoked morality in their opposition to the Iraq war or the government's refusal to sign the Kyoto Accord. It was John Kerry, who relied heavily on his moral convictions about the policy directions in the country during the debates.

Needless to say, there is some satisfaction in seeing those who think of themselves as so smart, so superior, representing a minority of the electorate. There is satisfaction in seeing all the millions George Soros spent to defeat Bush going down the drain. There is additional satisfaction in knowing that Hollywood celebrities will have to live with President Bush, unless, of course, they live up to their promises and leave the country.

Bush didn't merely win; he received a majority of the popular vote, something Bill Clinton could not achieve. He awakened the silent majority, who it seemed had been somnolent for a decade. Of the most significance, he embodied the spirit and common sense of plain folk.

It is precisely the arrogance displayed by the leftist fringe in the Democratic party that so estranged the voting public from the Kerry candidacy. In curious way the *New York Times* editorials, George Soros, Michael Moore, Barbra Streisand, et al., were unwitting allies of President Bush. His supporters rallied every time they expressed febrile denunciations of the president.

The campaign demonstrated that the blue states were likely to suffer the blues as long as the media and Hollywood elites attempt to speak for the Democratic party.

If anyone is asking-and I'm sure no one is-I would say what the Democrats need is a dose of country music, a sleepover in Indiana, some southern cuisine, a Nascar race,. and to vow not to read the *New York Times* even when it's delivered to their doorstep.

Two years after the Bush victory in 2004, however, the dust settled on the 2006 election and the chattering class voiced its view, largely cheerleading on behalf of the Democratic sweep. I offer a hard-headed assessment.

On the one hand, the Democrats took a page out the Newt Gingrich playbook by nationalizing the campaign. The one consistent theme was the "failure" in Iraq. That the war was going better than most people believe was overlooked. In this case, politics was national, not local.

Second, the Republicans didn't act like Republicans. They spent like Democrats, did not explain the purpose of the war effectively, and never connected Iraq to the global threat from the forces of darkness.

Third, the Republicans didn't take the gloves off. The idea that Rangel, Hastings, and Conyers, hard core leftists-with Hastings having been impeached for bribery-were omitted from the campaign. Republican revelations were impeded by the fear of the racist claim. Once again political correctness trumps national security.

Fourth, there is little doubt that the Rumsfeld resignation was related to the election result, notwithstanding claims to the contrary. A muscular foreign policy was in retreat with Baker and Gates placed on center stage. It is mind-boggling that Jim Baker believed Syria and Iran could be helpful in stabilizing events in Iraq. It's comparable to asking Stalin to stabilize Eastern Europe.

On balance, national security was less secure after than before the election.

The election also sent a message to the jihadists: The Americans cannot tolerate casualties. At some point, defeatism will triumph. This position will surely embolden the enemy as it did after the U.S. withdrawal from Somalia and the pathetically feeble response to the attacks on Khobar Towers and the *S.S. Cole.*

Each day violent forces in the Muslim world suggest that their willingness to embrace martyrdom gives them a distinct advantage over nations that value life and, as a consequence, are risk aversive.

Moreover, this election also made it difficult to engage in the surveillance necessary to thwart terrorist ambitions. Comments have already been made by Democratic leaders sympathetic to the ACLU that the Bush administration went too far in NSA wiretaps.

Of course, Nancy Pelosi, the new speaker of the House following the elections, and Hillary Clinton, the reelected New York senator, have tried to provide assurances that worries like mine are overdrawn. As Senator Clinton noted we are not "the 'cut-and-run' party but the 'stop-and-think' party." Perhaps. As I see it, after the Democrats stop-and-think, however, they will cut-and-run.

That the Republicans could not and did not make that argument is their shame. The nation is now more vulnerable to attack than ever before. Emotional resolve was eviscerated, a product of the naïve belief that if we leave Iraq the Middle East will be a peaceful area.

Struthious-like most Americans want to get off the foreign policy merry-go-round, but they cannot because history won't let them. Americans apparently don't want to fight, yet war has been declared against them and the enemy is not interested in negotiation or compromise. That enemy wants to destroy us. That is a hard lesson to imbibe.

We therefore assume things will be better with a House and Senate dominated by Democrats. Jihadists are bemused by this contention. To them killing a Democrat or a Republican is immaterial; they feel an obligation to murder infidels.

Tick-tock goes the clock for Americans impatient for results. The other side relies on the sands of time. History wails for a leader that can guide us back to reality, a leader who understands the global threat and is willing to counter it. Let's hope that person arrives before another major tragedy befalls the United States.

In the days leading to the 2008 election partisanship was in the air. Well-funded "attack dogs" sought to besmirch the reputations of the candidates, notwithstanding claims to the contrary.

The Democrats attributed the economic downturn to the Bush administration, soon to be described as "the Bush-McCain recession." By contrast, the Republicans said that Obama was inexperienced and an empty vessel without a record of accomplishment. Although there were unquestionably arguments to be made, both of these accusations missed the point.

There was unquestionably an economic downturn; it is not at all clear who was responsible for it. Blame falls on many parties, Democrats in the House of Representatives and several greedy folks on Wall Street.

It was true that Barack Obama had an unimpressive resume as a candidate for president, but whereas experience is something, it is not everything. Inexperienced candidates have occasionally emerged as competent presidents. It seems to me that the Republicans would have been better advised to concentrate on Obama's left-wing orthodoxy, a combination of redistributionist economics and transnational progressivism.

Senator McCain cleverly distanced himself from the unpopular Bush administration at the Minneapolis Convention. This was artful political legerdemain in which the party controlling the presidency was also leading a campaign for change.

To establish his *bona fides* as a foreign policy expert-clearly his weak hand-Mr. Obama said repeatedly we must disengage from or least draw down forces in Iraq and increase America's commitment to the stabilization of Afghanistan. It was the *surge*, that accounted for the remarkable improvement in the Iraqi campaign, a surge Senator Obama opposed. Is he now arguing that what he opposed in Iraq makes sense in Afghanistan? Is this an admission that he was wrong in the past or are the two campaigns unrelated in the senator's mind?

Political campaigns invariably seize on a theme. In most instances in American political history, there have been two themes: "four more years" or "it's time for a change." What distinguished this presidential season from those in the past is that both candidates saw themselves as change agents. Because change was in the political air, the real question was who of the two was prepared to bring it about.

To lend a degree of legitimacy for his change agenda Senator Obama borrowed the game plan from the 1992 Clinton campaign. At the time, Governor Clinton engaged in a drumbeat of lugubrious descriptions about the economy relying heavily on any story of woe or statistical downturn. He put President Bush on the defensive even though most of the claims were wildly exaggerated.

Senator McCain, by contrast, revisited the Reagan campaign of 1980. In that year, Governor Reagan argued that President Carter did not advance U.S. interests on the world stage using as evidence captive U.S. diplomats in Iran and an ineffectual reaction. McCain pointed out that his opponent is eager to engage in negotiation with some of the world's tyrants without preconditions, a sign of his immaturity and lack of sophistication. In fact, noted the McCain team, Obama believes negotiations are an end in themselves, not a process to achieve an end.

The amount of truth one attributes to these positions depends to some degree on a personal starting point. If you believed McCain could not free himself from the web of Republican politics, you would be inclined to believe in Obama's call for change. On the other hand, if you accepted the McCain contention that Obama was unprepared to lead a nation in parlous times, your vote would be with the senator from Arizona.

The real agents for change, however, were the marketers who sculpted these arguments into marble busts. Credibility is everything for average Americans, but it is often hard to know the authentic from the inauthentic in the era of spin doctors. Recognizing that distinction is the test for the voter, and obscuring the distinction is the challenge before the handlers.

The balloons were punctured and the lights dimmed. Delegates hurried off to various destinations in the nation. The residual effect of the 2008 Republican convention in St. Paul, Minnesota, however, will be felt for generations. This convention was different; the change Obama talked about was trumped by the change Sarah Palin embodied.

For at least a couple of generations the radical secularists have been gaining political ground in the United States. Their views are easy to categorize because they are the dominant opinions of media elitists: transnational progressivism, suspicion about the Judeo-Christian tradition, multiculturalism, a loss of confidence in American exceptionalism, and an acceptance of relativism.

Whether it was Hillary Clinton, Barack Obama, or almost any Democratic leader this radical secularist view has been their calling card. In 2006 Senator Obama gave a speech in which he cited "the myths in the Judeo-Christian tradition."

Even though Senator Obama discussed his "love affair with America" in his convention address, his memoir, *Dreams of My Father*[9], is devoid of any positive statement about American history.

In his Berlin speech Senator Obama said he is "a citizen of the world," yet his rights, privileges, and comforts are not derived from the United Nations or the International Court of Justice; they are conferred by his U.S. citizenship.

It is admittedly difficult to parse campaign political rhetoric from deeply held conviction and, despite my references, I do not have any intention of making partisan claims. What I am getting at is that this dominant secularist position was challenged in an unprecedented manner consistent with traditional American virtues.

Sarah Palin was everything Obama and Hillary were not. She didn't go to an Ivy League school; she was pro-life; she was pro-Second Amendment; she was for drilling, even in ANWR; she was suspicious of the Washington establishment; and she was a devoted Christian. These are the views and conditions radical secularists most dislike (vide: Oprah Winfrey and Maureen Dowd) and these are the conditions and views shared by the bulk of silent Americans.

It is not an exaggeration to suggest that Sarah Palin was a synecdochical heat-seeking missile sent by forgotten Americans, those Nixon called the "Silent Majority," at the very heart of elitist opinion. She was American to the core-home-spun, simple, tough. One might even describe her as someone out of the Jacksonian tradition.

For some she was easy to dislike, but she was the rising star in the party, and more significantly, the symbol of the forgotten American. In the culture wars where traditionalists have been on the defensive, she is a remarkable counter force-the voice of America that reasserts what makes this nation unique.

When delegates at the Republican convention shouted "USA," what they meant was "unify standards of America." Sarah Palin clearly sang that hymn. Like Senator McCain she is fiercely independent and, as she has now noted several times, doesn't care what the political establishment thinks of her. She talks and acts like Jimmy Stewart in *Mr. Smith Goes To Washington*, and, from what I can tell, has sent a shiver down the collective spine of the political elite. In the cultural battleground, tradition has reasserted itself, and from my perspective, it's about time. Contrast this condition with the "Obama factor."

I listened intently to Barack Obama when he delivered speeches. I observed him during debates. I watched as he was interviewed by news analysts. I frankly never understood Obamamania.

Mr. Obama speaks in empty platitudes. His cadence is reminiscent of preachers. His prescriptions can charitably be described as adolescent. He is remarkably self-absorbed and his wife remarkably bitter. He can be condescending as he was in his description of rural residents and defensive in describing his relationship with the Reverend Wright.

He sat in a Black Liberationist Church for twenty years listening to anti-American rhetoric never once protesting. In fact, he made a $25,000 contribution to Reverend Wright the same year the church honored Louis Farrakhan.

He is inexperienced. Six years as a backbencher in the Illinois legislature and four undistinguished years as a U.S. senator would in almost every instance disqualify a person for the nation's highest office.

He is reflexively liberal on every issue and achieved the dubious distinction of having the most liberal voting record in the Congress.

He has consorted with revolutionaries like Bill Ayers and Bernadette Dohrn, and has consistently lied about his ties to them.

This is merely the prologue to a general indictment. Even so, when all was said, he was the Democratic nominee, the hope for the future, and the person on whom the presidential fortunes of the party rest. How then did this unlikely scenario unfold?

As I see it, there were three central factors working in Barack Obama's favor. First, he was not Hillary Clinton. The party faithful were simply tired of the Clintons, their browbeating and sense of entitlement. Although some said a vote for Hillary was a two for one deal because you also got Bill; that in itself was enough to turn off many Democratic voters. Despite all the spin of her handlers, they could not conceal her vindictiveness and mean-spirited qualities.

Second, many voters eager for a change (an intentionally vague term) projected onto the Obama campaign the change they have in mind rather than the change Obama expresses. Perhaps that is why he speaks in platitudinous language. I have not yet met two Obama supporters who agreed on what his policy prescriptions were other than his desire to pull the troops from Iraq-a point on which Clinton and McCain agree, albeit with differing timetables, method and magnitude of withdrawal.

Third, perhaps most significantly, Obama was regarded as a national savior, the Superman arriving on the scene to clean up the mess created by the Bush administration. Whereas many saw him as a faux politician and a flawed person, others saw him as the great black hope-the man who could lead us to the promised land through his persuasive power and stentorian voice. It is not coincidental that this savior is black because the curriculum of multiculturalism has had a powerful influence on university graduates who speak in clichés and were trained in relativism and admiration for Third World cultures.

President Obama invariably asserts that he is seeking solutions for what ails the nation. He claims to be a pragmatist, a position confirmed by members of the press corps. Whether he realizes it or not, however, he has an ideological forebearer who has set the stage for this administration's agenda: Antonio Gramsci.

While still in his twenties Gramsci organized the Italian Communist party in 1921 with his colleague, Togliotti. Because this was four years after the Russian Revolution, Gramsci assumed Italians would welcome a Bolshevik convulsion of their own, but it didn't happen.

In reviewing the political landscape, Gramsci sought to explain why what seemed to him inevitable had not yet occurred. He found three explanations: Christianity, nationalism, and charity. As he explains in his writing the way to set the stage for a Marxist revolution was in coming to grips with these three conditions.

As a consequence, Gramsci converted Marxist economic theory into a cultural battle; as he saw it a march through conventional and normative institutions. The first stratagem was the assault on Christianity by arguing religion should not inform or be employed in public discourse. Gramsci realized that if religion were confined to private worship, its hold on Italians would dissipate. Hence, his arguments relied on science (more accurately scientism) and material claims devoid of references to the Church and its historic antecedents.

Second, Italians took great pride in their newly constituted nation, which was fifty years old in the 1920s. Gramsci contended Italians were part of a grand global mission, merely one story in the narrative of mankind. He therefore cleverly attempted to transform national loyalty into an abstract identification with human rights by describing patriotism as an anachronistic and childish fetish.

Last, Gramsci engaged in efforts to persuade Italians that the way, the only way, to express humanitarian concern for the poor or those left behind as the detritus of capitalism is through a government that can be benevolent and beneficent. For him, big government wasn't a temptation for tyranny, but rather the adjudicator for life's unfairness.

Whether recognized by President Obama or not, the parallels are striking. Although devoted to his own faith, President Obama through court decisions and his opposition to charitable trust programs has suggested overtly and tacitly that religion should be a matter relegated to private worship outside the confines of public life.

Second, the appointment of Anne Marie Slaughter to the Policy Planning Group and Susan Rice as ambassador to the UN argue persuasively that the president is committed to a transnational agenda, one that de-emphasizes America's global role and subordinates multinational institutions, such as the UN, as the primary channel of American foreign policy. Here is the John Kerry "global approval" position with a vengeance.

Last, through his proposal to deny tax deductions for charitable gifts, government is being converted into the only public charity. Moreover, the transfer of wealth in the stimulus package and the increased tax burden on the most productive element of society will inevitably decrease incentives and expand the size and influence of government.

History may repeat itself, but never exactly. I suspect that most politicians have never heard of Gramsci. I suspect as well that they would reject out of hand any parallel between a communist leader and an American president. What cannot be rejected, , is that President Obama is a product of American culture-an elite American culture cultivated by ideas at Harvard, Columbia, and the University of Chicago. That culture has been dramatically affected by the Gramscian march through our institutions.

The progeny of Gramsci are alive and well and now reside in the White House. They believe in big government, one worldism, distrust of religion, and a denial of American exceptionalism. Our leaders may not identify themselves as Gramscians and may even mock the designation, but make no mistake: Gramsci's DNA is in their bloodstream. Nonetheless, my hope is that despite the nation's political schism, Obama represented a postracial America.

At the outset of the new administration, there was a collective sigh of relief. Race as a campaign issue should have been permanently inserted into history's trash heap where it belongs. In that sense, there should have been justifiable rejoicing over what would be described as a new chapter in the national story.

As is the case with all presidents, however, once the applause ends, action is supposed to begin. And it did.

He proposed to Congress the Universal Health Care program based on the proposition that everyone in the nation must be covered by health insurance and, for those who for one valid reason or another are not, the government will insure them.

Of the most significance, however, Mr. Obama will focus on foreign policy with two overarching conditions in his telescopic lens: a timetable for withdrawal of American forces from Iraq and direct negotiations with Iranian leaders over nuclear weapons.

If the Obama campaign is to be believed, troop drawdown should have been completed within eighteen months.

Mr. Obama also indicated that he would engage in direct negotiations with Ahmadinejad about nuclear weapons and Iran's regional role. In fact, he noted these negotiations should occur without preconditions- an unprecedented development.

The question, of course, is what can President Obama say. Is he prepared to accept Iran as the area's most influential player with nuclear weapons? Can he offer blandishments that persuade Iran to forego the nuclear option? If he is not persuasive, what precisely would he be prepared to do? These questions suggest that negotiations between leaders without preconditions is unprecedented for a good reason: They cannot work and could put protagonists in a position where compromise is impossible. Needless to say, time is on the side of the party being asked to make concessions.

As I see it, the Obama presidency (based on campaign promises) should be obliged to: raise taxes across the board, make commitments for universal health care that will put enormous pressure on the budget, orchestrate a rapid troop withdrawal from Iraq that emboldens our enemies and invites further divisions in this beleaguered nation, and negotiate directly with Iran, which most probably results in a Persian empire with nuclear weapons.

It is customary for politicians to describe an issue that is important to them as a problem. After all problems require solutions and solutions are what get them elected. A politician will rarely, if ever, describe a "condition" because conditions occur in the natural order and aren't subject to positive intervention.

The Obama administration, however, has a new tactic, one that has raised the level of concern and the need for action. Every issue is described as a crisis. For example, we don't have an unemployment problem, we have an unemployment crisis. We don't have a healthcare problem, it is now elevated to a crisis.

Moreover, if it is regarded as a crisis, the government must act immediately. No time to delay. It is instructive that President Obama has noted that there is a deadline for healthcare reform. If the Congress does not comply, God only knows what will happen.

Chief of Staff Rahm Emanuel has said a crisis is too important to be wasted. It is surely a way to motivate the Congress to act. That is presumably why bills have been pushed through the byzantine process of lawmaking. It is obvious, however, that no one, including President Obama, read or had any idea of what was in the 1200 page stimulus package of $787 billion. Here was a bill designed to deal with the "unemployment crisis." When it was initiated unemployment was at 7.6 percent; after adoption unemployment escalated to 9.5 percent; however, that crisis-even more severe now-has been pushed aside for the healthcare crisis.

President Obama said if we do not act 47 million Americans without health insurance will be left floundering. The president unfortunately neglected to point out that no American can be denied medical treatment in a public hospital. He also ignored the fact that the large majority in the uninsured category earn more than $75,000 a year and could afford insurance but choose not to register. He also might have pointed out that a sizable number in this population are uninsured for a year or less, but if he were to say these things it would be hard to sustain the argument that there is a crisis.

Although there might be tactical value in claiming a crisis instead of a problem, there is a dangerous side to this claim. At this point President Obama lost his credibility. This tactic is like crying "wolf" every time an issue emerges. Even if there was a crisis, why would you believe this president?

Moreover, this tactic often confuses relatively manageable events with those that are intractable. As I see it, for example, healthcare insurance can be managed for a fraction of what the president has in mind if one were to realize there are about 8 million people without insurance who do not have the means to pay for it and require government assistance. By contrast, an Iran with nuclear weapons intent on using them to wipe Israel off the map may be a crisis-in-waiting if action isn't taken to thwart this eventuality. In the rhetoric used by the president, however, there isn't any distinction. Both are crises of seemingly similar magnitude.

In discussing North Korea's missile tests, the president employed strong language to chastise Kim Jong Il. He noted at the time that words must have meaning. Rather than use words as an empty gesture, the president insisted that his language be taken seriously. It is the president himself, however, who undermines this assertion with grandiose claims that are unrealistic or heightening the importance of issues with fear-laden terminology.

He must surely realize that not every matter that crosses his desk is a crisis. With a mindset of pushing legislation through ala FDR in the first 100 days of the New Deal, however, every matter is essential, every bill must be dealt with immediately, and every issue is a national crisis.

If, God forbid, a national crisis does emerge that requires mobilizing public support, a significant part of the population will say, "not again, this is simply another rhetorical exercise." If President Obama needs them, his rhetoric may push them away.

The results are in and my candidate lost the presidency. Because I love this country, I wish the President Barack Obama every success. This, however, was an election unlike any other. I don't think the Republicans merely lost an election, I believe many of us lost a country.

This was a land that once rewarded hard work and enterprise. A place where one's word was his or her bond. America was the land of opportunity. If you can't do it here, you can't do it anywhere. We were a people to be envied, both because we had the highest standard of living, and because we had the greatest degree of stability.

Americans were notoriously optimistic because we counted on tomorrow being better than yesterday. We were an open people dependent on fair play and a free market bounded by a standard of virtue. With all the blemishes in our past and breaches in our own ethics, we were a model of civic rectitude. "Dems that gives, gets;" those who wish to bilk the system will be discovered and isolated.

There was a time not so long ago when people did not depend on government to bail them out of financial difficulty, a time when the nanny state bred apprehension, not affection. Now, it seems, in the new America almost everyone wants a free ride. The non-taxpayer wants a rebate from the taxpayer. The poor man wants everything the rich man has and he wants the rich man to give it to him.

Enemies of the nation, it turns out, are not enemies at all; we merely defined them as adversaries. Had we been clever in the past, we could have defined them out of existence. All we have to do is engage in "soft power," diplomacy, and clever negotiating skill. Those who want to kill us will surely be persuaded that swords should be converted into plowshares. It's odd, but Osama bin Laden doesn't seem to embrace this position.

The America of "now" is one where that Orwellian logic rules. Redistribution of wealth is fairness. Taxes are patriotic. The free market should be a regulated market. Big government is good for you. Politicians know what kind of healthcare is best for you. Choice should be limited, except when it comes to abortion. Power comes from being powerless. Progressive education is designed to promote progress toward socialism. Race doesn't count unless a person of color tells you it counts. Higher education gets lower each year. Those who create our problems should be asked to solve them. Religion should be a private matter that does not inform public morality. Liberal is radical. Free speech is selective speech. Courage is impetuousness.

Yes, Americans-many Americans-want change. The level of dissatisfaction runs deep, but the national *cri de coeur* hasn't a direction. That's what makes it so dangerous. Americans live better than at any moment in our collective history, notwithstanding the meltdown on Wall Street, yet despair is ubiquitous. Observing 401K accounts disappear as soap bubbles admittedly will make anyone angry. Nonetheless, it is a privilege to live in the land of the free, a privilege now regarded as an entitlement.

It was once wrong to use community groups such as ACORN to steal an election. It was once wrong to conceal one's past in order to invent an identity. It was once wrong to use the instrument of government finance to satisfy a constituency and then claim an unregulated market is what ails us. It was once wrong to lie in a campaign and still is except when the media panjandrums avert their gaze for the lies of a favored candidate.

We surely face threats across the globe that cannot be easily forestalled. The most significant threat is arguably from within in the form of an unregulated government, a government large, intrusive, and seductive. This is the new American government that promises everything and demands very little from its citizens. "Shop until you drop" is the national anthem. After all, you don't have to fight if you don't want to and you don't have to sacrifice if that's too much for you. All you have to do is visit malls and keep opinions to yourself. Opinions are important because Truth Squads want to be sure you don't criticize the chosen candidate.

Where is my America, the place of fair play, individual rights, the rule of law and respect for private property? Was the past merely a dream from which I have awakened? Can that America of exceptionalism return? Can it find its way back into the public consciousness?

I have my doubts. Now the change agents scream "everything will be different." Alas, they are right. It appears as if everything will be different, most especially the end of an America I loved.

Still, immediately following the election Obama was an enigma, despite the fact he went through a grueling two-year campaign for the presidency. The sealing of his birth certificate, Columbia and Harvard transcripts, and even his baptismal certificate suggest he has something to hide; however, all of that is behind us now.

What lay ahead was another conundrum. Was Barack Obama a pragmatist who merely used affiliations with his church, community groups, and questionable friendships to advance his career or was he an ideologue who was influenced by Farrakhan, Ayers, Wright, Khalidi, and others on the hard left?

If the former, then many (most?) of the promises made during the campaign should have been postponed or forgotten. Realists in the Obama camp, even the Keynesians, know that raising taxes in a recession only exacerbates economic conditions. Likewise, an attempt to redress the structural dislocation of some workers by redrafting trade agreements such as NAFTA is the equivalent of a modern Smoot-Hawley tariff.

The question, therefore, was: Will Obama tack to the center or will he by nature, inclination, and association retain a redistributionist psychology? In most circles, there was the hope that Obama would be a dissimulator, put more politely, an opportunist who would say whatever is necessary to advance his position; however, this "optimistic" scenario suggests he will do what is necessary to retain power, but will not veer to an extremist stance.

On the other hand, there are constituencies in the Democratic party that got Mr. Obama to where he is and expect to be rewarded. Union leaders wanted to abandon the secret ballot; ACORN and other community groups expected to receive government largess; the teachers' unions expect significant allocations for education; welfare organizations expect tax standards that encourage "spreading the wealth around." These groups have to be mollified or an internal revolt in the Democratic party will ensue.

Would Obama steer a course between the Scylla of pragmatic policy decisions and the Charybdis of ideological commitment? Would this tension be addressed through some compromise or would it undermine his goals?

Because both the candidate and his policy perspectives were largely unknown, the resolution of this dilemma remained very much up in the air. Moreover, while President Obama displayed the temperament of a patient man during the campaign, it was not at all clear whether he would maintain his equilibrium in the White House when the pressure is far more intense than it is on the campaign trail.

In addition, would President Obama withdraw from Iraq in fifteen months as he promised or would intelligence estimates that suggest such an accelerated move trigger renewed violence jeopardizing the success achieved with the "surge?"

Again he was put on the horns of a dilemma, notwithstanding the obvious condition of the media giving him a free ride whatever he decides to do; however, expectations among his adherents ran high. A messiah is supposed to move mountains and divide the sea, not simply offer compromises even if those compromises are shaded by florid rhetoric.

This was not an easy adjustment for Obama. After the first year in the presidency, the fashionable racial argument has worn thin, political correctness is less valuable as a defense mechanism, and a public entranced by Camelot on Lake Michigan is searching for answers to tough questions.

One clearly hopes for the best and I certainly want to see Barack Obama succeed, but the questions looming ahead are tricky and the road to the future is filled with pitfalls.

On one matter there appeared to be consensus: bread and butter issues dominated the 2008 election and continue to dominate American politics. Contrary to the widely held opinion that youthful voters were caught in the whirlpool of Obamamania, it turns out they were principally concerned with the price of consumer products.

To my astonishment, the 18 to 25 year olds were not motivated to support Obama because of the war in Iraq or Oprah Winfrey's endorsement. It came down to the standard of living they either want or expect. So much for the new idealism.

As for older voters, the manifest opinion is that the Bush administration did not govern conservatively. Despite claims about fiscal responsibility, "compassionate conservatism" turned out to be big government programs, such as the prescription drug program, which resembled previous Democratic administration initiatives. Some voters argued that if the Republicans are 70 percent Democrats, why not vote for the genuine article.

It is instructive that Senator McCain, who was persistent in his opposition to earmarks and government spending, could not make the argument that he was better prepared to deal with the economic issues than his political rival. Nor could he make the case that the credit meltdown is directly related to political decisions made by Democrats. I would hazard a guess that perhaps 1 in 100 voters was aware of the Community Reinvestment Act and its insidious influence in providing uncollateralized mortgages to unqualified borrowers.

There were clearly other issues in the campaign. A majority of voters had a sense that the culture was moving in the wrong direction, but this was a vague feeling of unease overshadowed by the economic concerns.

The war against radical Islam and the attack on the World Trade Center and the Pentagon had similarly faded in the public consciousness. Americans take a great deal for granted, including their security. Neither the war nor homeland security played a critical role in this election, a curious testimonial to the Bush administration's success in Iraq and vigilance against terrorist threats.

On the matters that were emphasized by the public at large (e.g., spending, taxes, energy and the current economic crisis), a majority believed Obama and the Democratic party were in a better position to address these issues than their Republican counterparts.

Obama's ambiguous rhetoric apparently played well, notwithstanding the fact he will most likely raise taxes, increase spending on government programs, apply an expensive "cap and trade" policy on the energy bureaucracy, and continue the present commitment to adding government liquidity to the market.

To conceal his costly spending impulses, Senator Obama raised the specter of a tax rebate for 95 percent of Americans, a curious measure because at least 44 percent of the population does not pay taxes. McCain, however, remarkably did not take advantage of this obvious contradiction, mentioning it once in a throwaway line during the third debate.

What the opinion polls seem to suggest is that this election, like the 1992 election of Bill Clinton, was a referendum on the economy and McCain, willy nilly, was perceived as a proponent of Bush policies, which inaccurately were associated with the market downturn.

There was much handwringing in the Republican party about the loss. As I see it, refashioning perceptions of the party is necessary; however, the essential prescription is that when Republicans act like real Republicans they have an excellent chance of gaining public acceptance (i.e., adherence to limited government, sensible expenditures, and low taxes).

The key to future success is for Republicans to remember what led to success in the past and apply it to conditions in the present. Obama may be on the ascendancy at the moment, but political fortunes rise and fall. As Democratic policies fail-and they will-the Republicans should be poised to take advantage of the opportunity. This is the issue for Republicans: regroup, consider basic party positions, and organize them in a manner that the public will embrace.

As I mention Republican political strategy I'm reminded of what sets this country apart from others and what a president can do to accommodate various beliefs.

For example, U.S. troops stationed in Saudi Arabia to protect the Royal Family from terrorism are obliged to sail into the Red Sea in order to celebrate Christmas. This practice is designed to avoid any offense to their Muslim hosts.

Americans are so sensitive to the religious tradition of Muslims that crosses are covered up and any outward signs of Christian observance avoided.

Of course Muslim denunciation of Christians and Jews is widely accepted. On an Egyptian TV children's special, Jews were recently described as having "turned into apes" and the elderly of that faith "having become pigs." Christians are deemed infidels and the progenitors of the Crusades, a historical condition that for many Muslims has contemporary parallels. Iranian President Mahmoud Ahmadinejad recently said, "I will stop Christianity in this country."

With this as a backdrop, there is an American scene that deserves full disclosure. On December 6, I went to the White House Chanukah party. Jews from the most to the least observant were present. At the top of the stairs on the second floor the West Point Cadet Choir sang Chanukah songs in Hebrew. It should be noted that only about a quarter of those in the chorus are Jewish.

President Bush and Mrs. Bush greeted everyone with their usual cordiality. In fact, the president lit Chanukah candles and proceeded to tell the biblical tale of this celebration.

For me, however, the most startling scene occurred at about 8 p.m. Several Hasidic leaders noted that it was time for prayer. They sought a "minyan," a prayer group of ten males. Once assembled, these men proceeded to "daven." There they were, ten bearded men, bobbing up and down in prayer, in-of all places-the Dolly Madison room at the White House.

I could not conceive of a more incongruous scene. Here in what is ostensibly a Christian country, in a White House led by a born-again Christian, one can find Hasidim praying in the Dolly Madison room.

All I could say to my wife is, "only in America." I stood there frozen in astonishment. After all, Jews generally do not support this president. Of more significance, my mind kept returning to the intolerance Jews and Christians face in the Muslim world. How would the Muslim Brotherhood respond to this White House scene? In fact, who cares.

My heart swelled; I was simply filled with pride. Despite all the criticism from naysayers, despite all the braying from the left detractors, America is a magical place. You don't have to hide your religious beliefs; you can even display them in the White House.

Imagine, if you can, the response to a group of Hasidim that wished to pray in the Saudi Royal Palace. Their heads would be cut off before the first words were uttered.

The more I thought about this remarkable event and the contrast in the Muslim world, the more I came to realize what we are fighting to preserve and why this fight is so critical.

As I stood in the second floor corridor tears were rolling down my cheeks. Yes, I have a love affair with America. I love our history, our traditions, and our tolerance. I recognize national imperfections, but despite them, there isn't any nation in the world that can reproduce the prayer service I observed on December 6. That was the essence of America.

With the new year soon upon us I had only one resolution: a reasserted devotion to the land I love and a commitment to fight without restraint for its continued glory. This place is indeed the last best hope for mankind and those who don't realize it are merely blinded by ideological rage.

Perhaps it was hyperbole when Nathan Hale said: "I regret that I have but one life to give for my country." Hyperbole or not, that is the sentiment that should inspire us for the future. It is the spirit we need to sustain us. For doubters, I refer them to the scene I described in the Dolly Madison room. Only in America could it be found.

Chapter 8
Things Fall Apart

As the Iraq War resisted a quick resolution and casualties mounted, the partisan divide widened and rancor increased. The debate over the war provided a flashpoint revealing the irreconcilable differences between two worldviews competing for sway over the American society.

Theorists of war, from Sun Tzu[1] to Clauswitz[2], have recognized that the destruction of an enemy from within is as noteworthy as invasion from without. Moreover, the spirit, what might be described as the essential moral core of the state, must remain resolute to defend national interests against those who would destroy or conquer.

It is against this backdrop that I raise concerns about the war on terrorism and the rapid strides of radicalization in domestic life. In the interest of full disclosure, this concern emanates from an apparent complacency about domestic life evident among my fellow conservatives who have either forgotten the lessons of the culture war or choose to ignore them in their haste to fight foreign foes.

For example, David Brooks[3], author of *Bobos In Paradise*, seemingly ignores the deep-seated moral consequences of middle class financial analysts who go to S&M clubs in the evening. Several *National Review* editors contend homosexual marriages are virtually inevitable so there is little sense in resistance. Major conservative voices have been conspicuously quiescent about recent Supreme Court cases that have undermined equal treatment of the law and Judeo-Christian foundations of American life. Even President Bush who spoke out forcefully against race-based admissions policies in higher education, commended the Supreme Court for its decision to ensconce race as a central admissions criterion in the *Gratz* and *Gruder* cases.

This apathetic conservatism does not address whether the United States can sustain the will and cohesion to face its enemies when the very sinews of national purpose are being weakened. Stated another way: Can national will be mobilized when decadence and misguided radical ideas undermine the meaning and purpose of "the American idea"?

Mobilizing the nation to fight is always difficult after an event that outrages the public-such as the attack on the World Trade Center and the Pentagon-fades from memory. It is even more complicated when bread and circuses in the form of risqué TV programs are a national distraction, when the radical sensibility gains acceptance through homosexual unions or the now-common belief that whatever you do in the privacy of your home is acceptable. One might well ask: What are we fighting for? The right to watch *Sex and the City* and to legitimate gay weddings?

We have gone so far in the direction of expansive personal rights that a sense of duty is often overlooked. Don't get me wrong, I am an avowed believer in individual rights, but when a nation is at war-which is sometimes forgotten-it is necessary to marshal the requisite fortitude through the reassertion of national principles, which include the *raison d' etre* for America and its exceptional laws and conditions. The United States would be a different nation if it lost its religious foundation, the rule of law, a belief in private property, and, yes, individual rights.

The Founding Fathers didn't write a Constitution for the purpose of protecting MTV. There was a realization that we the people could have a republic if we could defend it, yet I wonder whether a self-indulgent, sex-obsessed popular culture isn't an enemy of national resolve. I wonder as well whether my conservative colleagues who once fought valiantly against the onslaught of decadence have thrown in the towel. More important, I wonder whether this aversion to the culture war will have an adverse effect on foreign wars.

My detractors might say, so far so good. We have titillating TV and a military capable of fighting brilliantly. We have lost the culture war, but we are winning the war on terror. Perhaps.

Will there come a time when a large portion of the nation loses sight of what it is defending? Can the conditions of personal license and the need for discipline, duty, and loyalty coexist?

I write with cautionary intent. I am surely not a Cassandra or an undeviating pessimist. In fact, American history is replete with examples of national resilience and I, like most Americans, harbor a faith in the future.

The departure from the past, however, may be that the voices that normally defend our traditions have been silent. Conservatives who have faith in preserving the best in our traditions are either on the sidelines cheering solely for the war effort or making concessions to cultural revolutionaries. They seem to have overlooked the nexus between internal moral strength and military muscle. They seem to ignore the manifold ways in which the acceptance of self-indulgent ideas can sap the resolution needed to fight.

The one overriding concern of the Founding Fathers was to create a nation steeped in liberty, open to peaceful change, and tolerant of diverse views. This might be called the liberal agenda for America.

Through wars and crisis, extremist claims, and passivity this liberal agenda was and remains the national credo. It is pledged in schools and defended in courts; it is sung with hand over heart and it is incorporated into the sinews of public debate.

Despite that, now, after the nation has been wantonly attacked, after terrorism's rancorous violence is openly on display, the harvest of liberalism's exercise must be examined.

I say this as a small "l" liberal who defends and relishes the openness America has granted me, yet at this moment I demur.

The vigorous assertion that arbitrary discrimination leads to the isolation of various groups and, alas, detention and death came with the Allied victory in World War II. A code of antidiscrimination laws emerged in the West that united liberalism's mission with the experience of the war. The code trampled other concerns leading eventually to the remarkable civil rights acts for blacks and ultimately for a host of other minorities facing cruel discrimination.

Of most significance, a form of categorical tolerance emerged that put almost any form of discrimination on the defensive. One can easily test this proposition by asking any group of randomly selected people to defend racial profiling.

Liberalism, has been forced to consider its inherent suppositions by defending those who would crush its beliefs and destroy the institutions that give it legitimacy. Of course, what I have been referring to obliquely is the defense of a radical form of Islam that is predicated on the destruction of the West.

After fighting World War II to rid the European continent of hate, hate rears its ugly head in the form of intolerance toward any infidels (i.e., Christians and Jews), and *mirabile dictu*, that hate is protected *willy nilly* by liberalism's institutions.

The obvious question that arises from this predicament is whether the West can defend itself against terror when the groups that foment it are protected by precedent and tradition. There is also the corollary question: Will the West be obliged to modify its essential credo to fight the internal war against terror? Perhaps one might ask if the West can modify its liberal beliefs to engage the enemy effectively.

Free speech is similarly based on the logical premise espoused by Voltaire that in the exchange of views truth might emerge. The emergence of truth is indefinite, just as speech may be imprecise and flawed, but unless free exchange is permitted truth has little chance of being uncovered.

Suppose, however, that speech is used not merely to promote a cause but to foment violence. Although free speech is not unlimited, after all one cannot advocate the overthrow of the government or shout "fire" in a crowded theater, it is possible to hide behind freedom of religion to pursue terroristic and hateful speech of a kind that is often found in many mosques. Here, too, liberal ideals collide with liberal survival.

Then there is freedom of association, the axiomatic contention that people should be free to create their own organizations, what Tocqueville so eloquently noted as one of America's mediating structures. From Lions' clubs to leadership groups, from Boy Scouts to the Young Presidents Organization, America has used the ability to associate as a mitigating force in a free market society in order to maintain communal bonds and charitable institutions.

What, then, does one do when this freedom is used to develop clandestine organizations intent on causing havoc and destruction? Can these organizations be penetrated by the F.B.I. when suicide missions are the goal? To what degree can civil liberties be constrained so that a modicum of security is preserved?

The answers are elusive. What is not elusive, of course, is the vulnerability created by liberalism's cherished beliefs. Does this scenario presage the end of the liberal experiment? That is doubtful. That, too, depends on whether terror occurs with frequency on our streets and whether civilization as we know it is at risk, to quote President Bush.

When Daniel Bell[4] wrote *The Cultural Contradictions of Capitalism*, he assumed that the libertarian impulses capitalism encourages would undermine the essential conditions of capitalism. It is instructive that the most significant impediment against a fight the United States and the West must pursue in order to defeat the forces of terrorism is also cultural.

Capitalism depends on a host of cultural values: sobriety, punctuality, hard work, resourcefulness, ingenuity, and the like. These characteristics, however, can easily be undermined by an ethos of depravity or, less ominously, relativism. Fighting a war similarly requires discipline, determination, honor, confidence, pride, and belief in a cause. These conditions can be challenged through creature comforts, lassitude, moral fatigue, and amorphous acceptance of internationalism. It is precisely these factors that must be resisted.

The evidence that resistance can be mobilized, however, is mixed. Americans want to win this war, indeed they know we must win this war, but they want it done without sacrifice. That has become the position throughout the West.

The Dutch, for example, are horrified at the ritual slaughter of the filmmaker, Van Gogh, but the government cannot mobilize itself to challenge homegrown Muslim gangs. Could it be that a society that legalizes drugs cannot marshal the will to protect itself from terror? Do cradle to grave welfare programs sap the individual drive for self-preservation?

In fact, do high-income, low-birthrate societies have the ability to absorb fatalities in war without losing the will to fight? Alas, it is a belief in the "softness" of the West that inspires radical Islamists.

At the risk of hasty generalization, it would appear that the secularization that haunts Europe has resulted in societies incapable of recognizing what Islamic radicalism represents and unable to defend themselves when the threat of terrorism is palpable. Complacency appears to be the handmaiden of appeasement.

On the other hand, the United States has found the will to fight, as the invasions in Afghanistan and Iraq demonstrate. Even here, however, where military culture is on the ascendancy, the culture is divided. The chattering class of *soi disant* intellectuals and readers of the *New York Times* editorial page are invariably opposed to the war in Iraq; in fact, this class is opposed to any war proposed by President George Bush.

In crass terms, a people who do not believe in anything enough to sacrifice invariably do not believe in anything enough to sustain life. Self-enhancement is not in itself a doctrine that inspires defense of civilization. If anything, the narcissistic impulse is atomizing, whereas the demands of national defense require social solidarity.

It is instructive that the culture is not merely different from the demands of war, but, in effect, it tends to contradict, to challenge the requirement of military mobilization. TV programming is obsessed with sexual promiscuity. Advertising has commoditized almost all human activity. Antireligious sentiment has superodinated self-absorption. Education tends to infantilize rather than encourage maturity.

It is hardly surprising that the military as an institution is one of the few that has the capacity to socialize boys into men. Assuming responsibility is increasingly subordinate to proclaiming rights. The young want freedom, but shun duty. These are clearly generalizations that I consider defensible, even as I acknowledge the existence of exceptions.

Almost all of American institutions promote the extension of adolescence. There are thousands of thirty year olds who act as teenagers. Guileless adults are preoccupied with themselves. Psychologists reinforce this trend as each person becomes a billboard saying, "look at me."

The question that surrounds this discussion is whether these self-indulgent types can be counted on to defend the nation against sanguinic terrorists intent on destruction. If only a minority defends the nation, cultural fracturing is bound to occur. The culture has a challenge: Marshal the spirit to unite the people behind a defense of the nation. So far, the culture contradicts military requirements. That is neither healthy for the body-politic, nor a sustainable position.

Just as the hangman's noose tends to focus the attention of the intended victim, war tends to reveal the true sentiment of its protagonists. What one sees on both sides of the Atlantic has a strong resemblance to history of the recent past.

In most respects, this history taught few lessons. Whereas it is axiomatic based on events in the 1930s that the path to peace is found in the preparation for war, Europeans seem immobilized, seemingly trapped by utopian vision and fear.

Memory of the German invasion of the Rhineland in 1936, accompanied by French and British inaction, has surely faded. Then as now the French believed in talk, not action, despite the fact that Hitler, by his own admission, would have retreated in the face of allied resistance-perhaps even forestalling World War II.

As the European reaction to American invasion in Iraq becomes transparently evident, it is increasingly apparent that France and Germany have descended into a Weimar syndrome characterized by decadence, socialism, peace at any price, and disarmament.

At home there is another curious historical analogy. The American Firsters of the Charles Lindberg variety who sought common cause with Communists that attempted to rationalize the 1939 Hitler-Stalin pact, railed against U.S. participation in the European war. This convergence of extreme left and right has reappeared with a vengeance. Pat Buchanan, in his own brand of American conservatism, is now in league with the diehard leftists like Ramsey Clark in denouncing the war in Iraq and suggesting that neoconservative Jews are responsible for the administration's strategy.

History clearly doesn't repeat itself exactly, albeit the parallels in this instance are eerie. While the world dithered, Hitler prepared his war machine for invasion; while the U.N. engaged in extended debate, Saddam Hussein has been working feverishly to enhance his geopolitical position. While Hitler violated the terms of the Versailles Treaty, Hussein violates- alas, had been violating for twelve years-the terms of the first Gulf War ceasefire promulgated by the U.N.

Even the rhetoric of anti-war demonstrators has the ring of the 1930s. From Paris to the east side of Manhattan vehement peaceniks call former President Bush "a cowboy," the same slur invoked by Adolph Hitler when referring to President Roosevelt.

It is unquestionably true that a free society should permit dissension. Opposition to the war should not be dismissed as the vacuous rant of the uninformed; however, the history of the recent past cannot easily be dismissed as a guide to the present. When the former president's detractors contend-as they usually do-that Saddam Hussein is evil and must go, they have an obligation to tell us how that can be accomplished.

At a meeting in New York a vigorous opponent of the war challenged my contention that the war was necessary. When I asked what he would do, he said, "We should reconceptualize." Somewhat confused by the use of this word, I inquired about his notion of reconceptualization. All he could mutter was "more diplomacy," ignoring twelve years of diplomacy and resolutions that did not alter by an iota conditions in Iraq.

This kind of response also has its historical analogy. When the proponents of peace in the 1930s were asked what can be done about Hitler, the common response was, "it's not our business," or let the Europeans settle this matter. Pearl Harbor offered a wake-up call. One might have assumed that 9/11 would have been a wake-up call for this generation, but apparently many are in a deep sleep.

For those who believe peace can be achieved by willing it, history has already passed them by. The march to the future is littered with the corpses of well-meaning people who refuse to consider the constraints of reality.

No sensible person wants war, yet were it not for Patton's troops in Europe, liberating those in concentration camps might never have occurred. The greatest liberation force in American history arguably was the Union Army that freed the slaves. It is facile to assert that war doesn't resolve anything. At times it resolves everything.

For those who take liberty for granted, who assume that history is merely a bad dream, the lessons of the past have little meaning. For those with a memory, it is self-evident there are times when there simply isn't a reasonable alternative to war.

When the statue of Saddam Hussein was toppled from its pedestal on the streets of Baghdad, all the negative predictions of the United States caught in a Middle East quagmire, with thousands of body bags and Iraqi resistance tumbled from the imagination of the war's detractors. There still remained a nagging question: How could so many pundits be so wrong? A corollary query was, why should the average person have a better grasp of historical forces than the well-educated editorial writers at the *New York Times*.

It isn't easy answering these questions, but it would be a mistake-in my estimation-not to try.

One condition is transparently evident: Worlds are made by metaphor as much as truth. For a considerable period intellectuals and *soi disant* intellectuals argued wittingly and unwittingly that "truth" is only what you believe. "I think it is true, therefore it is true," has become the calling card of the chattering classes from Berkeley to Greenwich Village.

The children of a narcissistic era are persuaded that subjectivity, which often takes the form of a self-described utopianism, is what ultimately counts. The consequence was that arguments about weapons of mass destruction, tyranny, and torture are relegated to "opinions" that may or may not be authentic. The argument always seems to return to "what ought to be."

Second, the elites in this society, privileged beyond compare, assumed-based on their educational experience-that the United States was invariably wrong. They responded instinctively to every presidential statement as if it was former President Nixon lying about Watergate. Moreover, many in this group were still fighting the Vietnam War. They were the self-appointed bold resisters saving the country from itself. Try, as one might, to persuade this group of true believers that Iraq is not Vietnam won't work. Intellectual blinders won't permit the sunshine of true debate.

It was instructive that the heroes for these detractors are invariably those who resisted government entreaties, whether it be Martin Luther King, Daniel Ellsberg, or Woodward and Bernstein. Hence, those who supported government action are *ipso facto* objects of suspicion. It is not surprising that Edward Said[5], Columbia University professor and activist in behalf of Palestinians, defined an intellectual as "a dissenter."

On the moral front elites had been fed a pabulum of American venality. Right and wrong had been put in the cauldron of semiotics. For the hard core leftist, President Bush, not Saddam Hussein, was the tyrant. Here is Orwellianism American style. No matter how good the news, those immersed in this mindset will find a justification to hate the nation.

When American troops entered Baghdad and Iraqi people were parading through the streets carrying American flags and kissing portraits of President Bush, an American leftist was asked about the scene. He said, "Don't be deceived; these people are happy to see Hussein defeated, but they aren't happy about the Americans in their country." It might well be asked who is really deceived. Even when Iraqis thank Americans for their liberation, it will not satisfy those blinded by antipathy to the Bush administration.

Here were the products of the revolution in thinking launched by Gramsci. Gramsci realized that if you can alter political concerns from individual rights to a categorical imperative, institutions would reform in a direction he considered desirable. To a surprising degree he was right. For example, witness the widespread shift from individual merit-the hallmark of the early Civil Rights movement-to affirmative action or group privilege.

The same condition prevailed on the international front where we saw that many demonstrators were willing to sacrifice America's national sovereignty for U.N. authority as if this international body possessed a legitimacy unavailable to the United States. For some a constituent body composed of tyrants and fiends as well as constitutional governments curiously had more standing than the most successful republic the world has ever known. Then again, they were made myopic by the metaphorical world their imagination and ideology fashioned.

The issue at hand is how to convince a portion of the population about anything when they are resistant to logic or reason. There is nothing you can do but rely on the dominant forces in history. Whenever people have the ability to choose for themselves they display a preference for free markets, constitutional authority, the rule of law, and individual rights. Even the hard core radicals may one day imbibe that lesson, but I'm not holding my breath. What the antiwar movement has unleashed, however, is worrisome.

At this time of war and contentious claims raw sentiment is often palpable. Words can be hurtful. They reveal feelings long held dormant.

This was nowhere more apparent than in a May 7, 2004, column for the state newspaper of Columbia, South Carolina, by the eighty-two-year-old Senator Ernest Hollings[6]. In this piece Hollings accused President Bush of invading Iraq "to secure Israel" and "to take the Jewish vote from the Democrats."

He argued that former Assistant Secretary of Defense Richard Perle, Deputy Defense Secretary Paul Wolfowitz, and syndicated columnist Charles Krauthammer, all of whom are Jewish, were trying "to guarantee Israel's security."

Senator George Allen of Virginia, Senate Republican campaign chairman, accused Hollings of making "anti-Semitic, political conspiracy statements." Despite several opportunities to recant, Hollings refused to do so.

Hollings, of course, is not alone. The Internet is filled with innuendo of precisely this variety. For a distinguished senator to make comments of this kind, however, is truly remarkable.

The anomalous nature of his statement is evident in the 1998 legislation proposed by the Clinton administration and passed by the Congress for the replacement of Saddam Hussein and the pacification of Iraq. Senator Hollings supported this act.

Is it possible that the same view about Iraq has different partisan meaning? Is it possible that Hollings challenged the Bush decision because of what he considers the Jewish architects of the war within and without the present administration?

On any level, the Hollings comments are simply preposterous.

Richard Perle does not have a position in the Bush administration. Paul Wolfowitz does not have authority to make administration policy unilaterally. Charles Krauthammer is not William Randolph Hearst declaring, "you make the war and I'll make the headlines."

It should also be noted that a secure Iraq may remove one of Israel's many Middle East enemies, but it does not assure her security, as any daily reading of newspapers can attest.

Last, the idea that Bush called for the invasion of Iraq in order to obtain the Jewish vote is a calumny that goes well beyond hardhitting political exchange. Moreover, even if Bush did receive the Jewish vote, the numbers are certainly not large enough to be decisive. If Bush did exceedingly well with Jewish voters in 2004, however, he was still unlikely to get more that 40 percent of that vote, a high water mark approximated by Reagan in 1984.

What Hollings' view reflects is a reflexively anti-Jewish belief so common among anti-Semites. Paranoia is evident along with attributions about Jewish power and behind the scenes influence.

This Hollings statement is a rather strange way to conclude a thirty-eight-year Senate career. He has created a political tsunami that could threaten future elections in South Carolina and possibly the national elections as well. Inez Tenenbaum, the Democratic state education superintendent and designated Hollings successor, is already on the defensive.

While anti-Semitism has raised its ugly head in the Middle East and Europe, it has been quiescent in the United States. I'm convinced the Hollings' statement was aberrational; nonetheless, it is important to lance the boil of this miasma. Whatever Hollings reputation may have been, it's time to repudiate his words unequivocally.

It is irrelevant whether he decides to express remorse. He has opened a Pandora's box of discredited opinion that hasn't any place in polite society. "It cannot happen here" has happened. It's now necessary to make sure it doesn't happen again.

"Never again," however, has become "yet again" as the war against Islamism unfolds.

Whereas there were those in the United States during the Cold War who tried to stifle criticism of communism, criticism went on largely unabated. There were those whose style and scattershot approach offended, viz. Senator Joseph McCarthy. There were the heroes and heroines, however, who understood the nature of the enemy and fought brilliantly with scathing indictments (e.g. Midge Decter, Irving Kristol, Sidney Hook, Gertrude Himmelfarb, Stephen Spender, and Norman Podhoretz).

The United States faces a new, formidable challenge from radical Islam, or what some have called Islamofacism, at the onset of World War IV, but curiously the rules have changed. Free speech surely exists, and just as surely radical Islam has come in for criticism; however, it is unique that whatever the critique, Islamists cry Islamophobia, a presumptive claim of bias or, perhaps worse, reflexive prejudice.

This claim has resonance, in part because there are sectors of the society that believe it, there are occasional lapses into generalizations, and there are defenders of religion who equate Islam with the Judeo-Christian tradition and view any criticism of the faith, even when it applies to radicals, as an assault on Islam generally.

In a curious way the First Amendment is an instrument for Islamists as well as a barrier against them. The Islamists use it as antitoxin against what they conceive of as unfair criticism launched to undermine the faith. After all, they note, doesn't the First Amendment allow for the free exercise of religion?

On its face, this is a valid claim; however, the First Amendment is not a pact for self-annihilation. When Islamists claim infidels-non-Muslims-must submit or die and this is preached in some mosques across the country, the protection of religious freedom seems questionable.

It occurs to me that what is tantamount to calling for insurrection should not be tolerated no matter what legal protections seemingly exist. Of course, these matters must be addressed by the courts. First, I believe they should be addressed in the court of public opinion.

Americans should know what they are up against. They should understand as well that our rights can be perverted in that almost Orwellian way. They should appreciate that legal issues can be used to erode self-confidence and break down the moral fortitude so necessary in this struggle.

Can you imagine the consequence of communophophia during the Cold War? Some apologists certainly raised this banner, but it did not gain traction. Had it been in the ascendancy, we might be speaking Russian today or, to put it less boldly, communism would have gained sway throughout the world.

That is the rub at the moment. The internal struggle to accommodate and simultaneously oppose radical Islam weakens national resolve. How do you oppose a condition you are obliged to countenance? How do you endorse a movement trying to undermine the country?

How these questions unravel remains to be seen, but on one issue there isn't any question: The present state of affairs is causing great frustration and anguish for many Americans and, for some, has even shined a bright light on the manner in which basic rights can be twisted and used against us.

The avatars of moral equivalence, who found themselves comfortably ensconced in op. ed. pages during the Cold War, have discovered a new battleground. Although the balancers of moral concerns certainly exist in the United States, most of the contemporary generation for this phenomenon resides in Europe. These people are obsessed with one issue: the war in the Middle East.

Faced with this conflict, the avatars of moral equivalence (AMEs) shy away from the resolute punishment of those in the wrong and insist that both sides have "legitimate issues" that need resolution. There are surely Palestinian issues wrought by Arafat and his benefactors in the Arab world. To suggest that these issues are comparable to the wanton murder of innocent people in Israeli towns and cities, however, is comparable to the difference between a firecracker and a neutron bomb.

The universalistic impulse of AMEs implies a logic that dictates terrorists and victims must be treated alike in the so-called peace process. Both parties-contends the large majority of European commentators-must learn to abandon their "intransigence" in seeking resolution.

By placing aggressors on the same moral plain as victims, however, AMEs deny both right from wrong and Israelis the right of self-defense.

Although the conflict may seem unfair to the uninitiated because Israelis possess the technical means to retaliate against attack and the Palestinians rely on suicide bombers and stones, overlooked in this equation is that Palestinians invariably attack first.

As Shakespeare noted in *Othello*, he who inspires jealously and hatred is also responsible for vengeance. From a moral standpoint the people who inspired the attack on innocent Israelis are also responsible for the innocent Palestinians who may die when retaliation occurs. Despite all the verbal gymnastics now being employed by the European press, Sharon is not Arafat.

The hear-no-evil, see-no-evil AMEs view of the Middle East, however, is a variant of multiculturalism, which assumes all cultures are mirror images of one another. Hence, one finds hypersensitivity to Islamic (the "underdog") concerns and an insensitivity to Israeli concerns, with Israel seen as a surrogate for the American imperium. That there may be genuine issues of right and wrong in this calculus is overlooked.

Conflicts everywhere on the globe are seen by AMEs as a Manichean struggle between imperialist oppressors and the wretched of the earth. Complexities don't exist. With this mindset, the bloody actions of Islamic radicals are tolerated, alas, even admired. Just as Castro was once depicted as that romantic revolutionary fighting from Cuban hills against a corrupt regime, the neo-romantics have invested suicide bombers with the same attribution. Rather than call these fanatics mass murderers-which they are-the Europeans press corps usually refers to them as "martyrs for a good cause."

International lawyers in Brussels called for a "war crimes" trial against Ariel Sharon, yet were conspicuously silent about the crimes of Yassir Arafat. The U.N.-sponsored anti-racism conference in Durban excoriated Zionism, but left radical Islam unmentioned.

AMEs clearly prefer therapy over discipline. They wish to purge their demons without recognizing the consequences of or the complexities in global actions. They are members of a therapeutic generation eager for a psychological resting place, but morally obtuse.

These people, unfortunately for Israel, aren't going away. The best that one can hope for is that victory in this Middle East war will shift their gaze to a new battleground similar to the way they responded to the U.S. victory in the Cold War.

Still, the ideological battlefront must be considered as well.

It is always interesting to observe how postmodernist thinkers can engage in verbal convolutions before they find themselves in a tangle.

On October 15, 2001 in the *New York Times* Stanley Fish, noted author and dean at the University of Illinois, argued the case for postmodernism after the September 11 attacks. According to critics, postmodernists denied the possibility of objective description, thereby leaving one with no firm basis for condemnation of the terrorist attacks.

Professor Fish contended that "the only thing postmodern thought argues against is the hope of justifying our response to the attacks in universal terms that would be persuasive to everyone, including our enemies."

He went on to note that "universal absolutes" only confuse the situation. Quoting Edward Said of Columbia University, Fish shunned such "false universals" as "the face of evil," "irrational madmen," and "international terrorism," which obscure a purposeful agenda.

Professor Fish contended that Reuters was correct in the care it exercised over the word *terrorism*. After all, "one man's terrorist is another man's freedom fighter." The word lacked refinement and therefore, according to Fish, it obfuscated "a better picture of where we are and what we might do."

In the end, Fish maintained that relativism, which is the embodiment of postmodernism, meant "putting yourself in your adversary's shoes, not in order to wear them as your own, but in order to have some understanding (far short of approval) of why someone else might want to wear them...." This, he suggested, is "simply another name for serious thought."

There are many things one might say about the Fish analysis, but serious thought is not among them.

Let me offer a universal term that doesn't equivocate: *evil*. I would argue that terrorists and freedom fighters in the cauldron of postmodern exegesis might be confused. For those inoculated against these ravings, however, the distinction is simple. Freedom fighters do not internationally engage in the wanton killing of innocent people.

When roughly 3000 people were killed in the World Trade Center for no other reason than they went to work, that is the face of evil, and, yes, I'm persuaded the universal definition applies.

Should I empathize with a crime so dastardly? Even if I understand the rage surrounding the attack, I still cannot understand the act itself. There is a distinction Fish ignores between understanding a motive and still not understanding the act emanating from it. I may hate a colleague for what I consider justifiable reasons, but the hate cannot serve as a rationalization for murder.

The problem with Fish's relativism is that it ignores a certain reality even he at some point must recognize. If someone decides to slit his throat with a razor would Professor Fish ask why this would-be murderer is about to commit such an act? Would he attempt to understand the motives of the killer or would he strive in every way possible to prevent his death?

The answer is obvious. It is also obvious, notwithstanding Fish's ramblings, that society has a responsibility to preserve itself against those who would choose to destroy it. That is a universal contention that I believe to be true.

Professor Fish believes that if motives are understood and a place defined one can at least try to anticipate future assaults. But is this point accurate? The motives surely are known: real and imagined grievances. It is just as certain that the places are known: Afghanistan, Syria, Iraq, Iran, Saudi Arabia, Egypt, Gaza, and the West Bank. Now what?

This argument is mere subterfuge for the central postmodernist view that we don't know what we mean when universal terms are used. In the September 11 attacks I maintain Americans were not the least bit confused about terminology. We saw the face of evil; it did not require an interpreter.

Those who died at the World Trade Center were innocent men, women, and children. In my judgment there isn't any explanation that warrants those murders. End of argument.

There is little doubt that the nation was divided over the war in Iraq. If television news offers a partial glance at public opinion, there was vocal opposition to President Bush's position, but this was certainly not an equal distribution of opinion. I would guess that the president outnumbered his opponents by at least a margin of 3-to-1.

Nonetheless, news directors gave half their air time to the president's detractors. Every demonstration was covered. TV personalities, who opposed the war from Peter Jennings to Peter Arnett[7], became the focus of stories. It is instructive that reporters were no longer obliged to report, but become the center of news stories. Geraldo Rivera actually believed his daily commentary was more important than news of the war.

It is not only narcissism or inflated egos at play. It is truly reprehensible that many of the naysayers wished to see America defeated or, at the very least, embarrassed. It is not coincidental that during his interview on Iraqi television Peter Arnett said: "On reports about civilian casualties here, about the resistance of the Iraqi forces, are going back to the United States. It helps those who oppose the war when you challenge the policy to develop their arguments."

Nor is it coincidental that a Columbia anthropology professor stated publicly that he hoped the American forces would face many Mogadishus.

In the mind of many dissenters there was an overriding belief that the United States was evil-beyond redemption-and the rest of the world, particularly the third world, was basically good. In truth, of course, the United States is unique in its beneficence and charity, and most of the third world is dominated by tyrannical and corrupt leaders. If your experience is limited to a university classroom, however, this upside-down version of reality is not surprising.

After all, this is the land of the free in which diverse opinions are tolerated. Saddam Hussein has both eliminated dissent in Iraq and quashed any hint of disloyalty, yet that condition has little influence with American dissenters whose hate America first message is their preoccupation.

Closing the gap between the pro- and anti- positions is quite impossible.

Because America is the embodiment of evil in critics' eyes, there isn't any claim that will satisfy their opposition to the deployment of armed forces. This clearly isn't the view of all critics, only those who are most extreme. It is important, however, for sensible critics to dissociate themselves from extremists, a recommendation easier to consider abstractly than in practice.

If there is an ideological divide-a case that appears incontrovertible-the side you are on is more significant than who stands with you. Positions, however, are credible because of their advocates. For example, I find it hard to take seriously any criticism expressed by erstwhile Attorney General Ramsey Clark because his institutional funding comes from rogue states in the Middle East.

It is important to consider the agendas-both revealed and concealed-on both sides of the divide, yet one thing should be clear: however imperfect the United States may be, it is the most exceptional nation on the globe and one that should be given the benefit of the doubt.

That doesn't mean the United States is always right or that criticism shouldn't be considered. What it does mean is that a nation at war deserves heartfelt support from its people, even if the policy that brought us to this point is questioned.

This is a curious era, a time when celebrity status trumps sound judgment; when many individuals think of themselves as more competent to make decisions than elected leaders. That said, it is remarkable that the vast majority of Americans stood with the former president, despite the nightly barrage of anti-American sentiment on the news. Perhaps Americans heard, but did not listen or perhaps common sense inoculated them against absurd commentary. Whatever the case, I'm proud to have stood with America's majority.

Listening to the American tourists traveling in France, it is apparent we are in the "age of Obama." The Ugly American has morphed into the Apologetic American, the one who is sorry for everything. This American apologizes for breathing French air; for being colonists; for appearing arrogant.

It is hard to fathom how this new American can apologize to the insufferable French for arrogance or colonialism, but there you have it. American tourists merely ape their president. In this period, Americans are unequivocally sorry.

Now in order for these tourists to appear genuine, they must impose historical amnesia on themselves. Forget the role nineteen- and twenty-year-old soldiers played in liberating France during World War II. Forget American blood that seeped into the sands at Normandy. Forget the Marshall Plan that rebuilt war-torn France. In fact, forget much of the twentieth century.

Rewrite history so that the French appear as sophisticates and Americans hopelessly "nouveau arriviste." You must rewrite this history, and it must be rewritten by the Americans themselves. They will be their own revisionists.

From any point of view, this is sickening. The American apologist has nothing for which apology is necessary. If anyone should be bowing and offering thanks it is the French. When a Frenchman recently upbraided Americans for only speaking English, he should have been reminded that were it not for Americans the French would only be speaking one language as well, German.

I admit that the French generally know more about wine than Americans, but when it comes to manners, what the French call, "politesse," Americans generally beat them at their own game.

Every time an American apologizes for Vietnam or "wrecking the Atlantic alliance" (to quote President Obama) I want to slap him into sensible thought. It was the French who left Vietnam with their tail between their legs and Presidents Eisenhower and Kennedy who bailed them out.

It was De Gaulle who refused to join NATO and demanded a "force de frappe," a toothless response to Soviet nuclear threats. It is the United States that is responsible for putting teeth in the European fighting force. President Obama has given impetus to the contemporary French argument that the United States may not be so bad after all. This is an America, however, that refuses to flex its military muscle; an America that appears confused and without direction. If one can find a stance in the new administration, it is the accommodative spirit that cannot distinguish between an enemy and a friend. It is an America that says pleasantries about Iran and castigates Israel. It is an administration that wants to turn back the clock in its dealings with Muslim nations, but refuses to mention the sacrifices Americans made for Muslims in the Balkans and Iraq, among other places.

Although it is an unpopular position, I prefer the Ugly American to the Apologetic American: the one wearing the horribly garish Hawaiian shirt, the one who brags about American accomplishments, the person who knows America bailed out France and isn't afraid to say so, the one who interred political correctness, and the one who refuses to apologize for American actions. Americans sacrificed blood and treasure for Europeans. That is nothing of which to be ashamed.

As I see it, we need a dose of Yankee-first patriotism. That surge of nationalistic fervor might do us some good and might even have a chastening effect on the French (Notice, I said *might*).

It is strange that I long for the Ugly American I once criticized, but whenever I hear the Apologetic American on the Champs Elysee, I only wish the past can be resurrected. Give me the Ugly American any day of the week rather than this contemporary counterpart.

This is surely not an Ugly American, but this is an American with a clear and present agenda and an influential role in the Obama era.

On the other side of Yankee patriotism is a self-styled radical who happens to be a billionaire.

Who is George Soros and why is he saying such awful things? Most Americans do not know this billionaire investor, but he, using his vast wealth, has become a force in left-wing political circles. In some ways, he is the litmus test for Democratic politics.

Most of the time, Mr. Soros concerns himself with foreign affairs pointing out what he considers the failures of the Bush administration. In interviews with the press, Soros claims that President Bush's war on terror "is really exploitation." Moreover, he urges European leaders to adopt a stance different from the United States.

Writing in the London based *Independent* Soros[8] contended the Bush foreign mission shamelessly exploits fears generated from 9/11. As he saw it, "fear is a bad counselor; we must resist it wherever it comes from." He maintained that with the Bush policy terror will never end. "The terrorists are invisible; therefore, they can never disappear. It is our civil liberties that may disappear instead."

That position is the *sine qua non* of leftist thought. Terrorism is merely a cover for a subtle *coup d'etat* in which civil liberties are imperiled. According to Soros, we exaggerated the threat al Qaeda represents and underestimated the extent to which civil liberties are at risk. For him terrorism is an abstraction representing different forces and groups that require correspondingly different means of engagement.

When it comes to the issue of Iraq, Soros takes a pass. He expresses concerns about minority groups in that country, but he doesn't know how we should help them. That doesn't translate into a diatribe against the use of military force, but when force is mentioned it is accompanied with the caveat "where appropriate." Of course, where it is appropriate is rarely, if ever, explained.

Soros believes there are "nefarious psychological reasons" that explain the behavior of Bush-Cheney, but these are also never specified, albeit he has called erstwhile Ambassador to the U.N. John Bolton a member of a group of "rabid American supremists." Does that mean they are patriots?

Soros seems to take great pleasure in attacking members of the Bush administration in a manner reminiscent of Michael Moore. For example, on one occasion he said, "you don't have a Karl Marx, you have only a Karl Rove who has been successful in creating a coalition of fundamentalists."

In Soros' book, *The Age of Fallibility*[9], it is noted that after 9/11 when President Bush said, "Either you are with us or you are with the terrorists," Soros was reminded of Nazi propaganda. Although he attempted to backpedal on this outrageous claim, he did say, "The Bush administration has been able to improve on the techniques used by the Nazi and the Communist propaganda machines by drawing on the innovations of the advertising and marketing industries."

In an article published in the *New York Review of Books*[10], Soros asserted that America should pressure Israel to negotiate with the Hamas-led unity government in the Palestinian territory regardless of its refusal to recognize the right of the Jewish state to exist. Mr. Soros goes on to say that the overarching reason the United States has not embraced this policy is the insidious influence of the American Israel Public Affairs Committee, an argument reminiscent of the Walt-Mearshimer thesis.

The Soros article puts Democrats in the awkward position of having to choose between Soros, a major funder of its causes, and the pro-Israel lobby, whose members are disproportionately represented in the Democratic party.

In a sense even Karl Rove, as bright as he is, couldn't have invented George Soros. He is the leftist that keeps giving, both to the causes he wants to support, and to those he detests. Imagine a megalomaniacal billionaire intent on destroying a democratically elected president with well-oiled propaganda institutions he subsidizes and with outrageous commentary he glibly delivers to the press.

Soros thinks he funds public interest organizations, but in fact they are ideologically driven propaganda enterprises designed to foster his belief system. Some on the left have denounced Soros and his campaigns, but one shouldn't underestimate the lure of Soros money and what it can buy. He has become the principal philanthropist for radical groups and, if money talks, Soros should be heard from for a very long time.

With the Republican Convention only a few months away and with news of bloodshed in Iraq on the front page of newspapers, the ground was set for demonstrations by so-called antiwar protestors.

The words *so-called* are employed because the organizers of these events were invariably the same set of characters who reflexively appeared at all the protest movements. These are the well-funded opponents of the putative establishment who as our Constitution indicates are protected by the First Amendment.

They are not protected, however, from valid criticism leveled against them. There is much to be said on this score.

The Union Square organizers of "peace" protests were led by Ramsey Clark, former attorney general, and his posse of radical ideologues. Many in this group were former members of the Communist Party of the United States (CPUSA). ANSWER (Act Now to Stop War and End Racism) is the largest of these umbrella organizations put together after 9/11 to organize anti-U.S. protest activity. It works hand in glove with I.A.C. (International Action Center), which has a long and sordid history as an apologist organization for Stalinist crimes and as a defender of North Korea and Castro's Cuba. So much for the claims of peace.

ANSWER called for the impeachment of President George Bush on the charge that he chose to attack both Afghanistan and Iraq without provocation, violating their sovereignty and "executing thousands of men, women and children in the process." Here is the pretext for disrupting the Convention. Plans were underway to bring as many as 500,000 demonstrators to New York during the August 29 to September 4 period.

Not to be left out, the New Left now represented by NION (Not In Our Name) planned to launch rallies of its own. Included in this group are the usual suspects: Tom Hayden, Noam Chomsky, Howard Zinn1, Al Sharpton, Oliver Stone, Ed Asner, Martin Sheen, Danny Glover, and Ed Harris, among others. This group was inspired by the former SDS (Students for a Democratic Society) and the Black Panther Party and is organized to oppose all U.S. security interests.

Old Left and New Left were united behind the well-worn bromides of the past: "U.S. colonialism," "genocidal warfare," "blood for oil," and "trampling on liberty for profits." Because the Democratic Party Convention of 1968 was the apogee of this protest movement, the new popular front planned to attempt a dramatic reprise. History often repeats itself as caricature.

The leftist policy prescriptions of these groups were also part of retread culture: cutting-if not eliminating-defense spending, reliance on the U.N. for worldwide peacekeeping, emphasis on the World Court for the adjudication of national differences, and assistance for any nation or group of nations that can cripple U.S world dominance.

Complicating this scenario are many legitimate liberal organizations that would be drawn into the protests because they share some part of the general agenda or simply because they wanted to see President Bush defeated in the 2004 election. The American Civil Liberties Union and the Ford Foundation immediately come to mind as falling into this category.

This army of dissension could have disrupted the Convention and could have derailed U.S. war objectives, albeit both were unlikely, if plausible, possibilities. The prospect of clashes between police and protestors could have affected the 2004 election, although in which direction isn't obvious. Riots in 1968 at the Democratic Convention had an effect on Nixon's victory.

It would appear that the nation shares the president's antiterror campaign, but bloodshed on the streets of New York might have a chastening influence on voters. It should be clear that the left is poised to cause as much chaos as possible. For those who have been through this before, it isn't a new story, but it doesn't seem as if this story will ever end.

Epilogue

There is a shift occurring in the United States, a tectonic shift that is imposing statism in a land predicated on limited government.

In the past, the not very distant past, mediating structures served as a barrier against managerial despotism. These structures, however, have been under assault for decades and are showing signs of weakness and decay.

The family has been undermined by divorce and illegitimacy. Schools have eroded rigor and standards. Churches resemble social institutions more than religious centers. Associations like Rotary and Lions are suffering from insufficient enrollment and a lack of interest.

The America Tocqueville described in mid-nineteenth century is largely gone, a testament to the past when national identity was being refined. The New Hampshire slogan, "Live free or die," is great for license plates, but not for contemporary politics.

Some would argue that big government is a natural consequence of living in a bigger and more complex nation than was the case 100 years ago. Needless to say, this is obvious. It is not so obvious, however, that incrementally the government has assumed the position of granting rights to citizens instead of having citizens grant rights to the government. During this onset of the recession it was believed by members of both parties that extending government power was essential in dealing with the economic vicissitudes of the moment. In doing so, however, the politics of grievants has emerged. If the government uses its largesse to address social woe how are rights determined and who allocates the benefits? A government insistent on hand-outs will be a government that encourages grievance.

Let me not overstate the case. Despite an inclination to support limited government as the nation's founders did, my issue with the Obama administration, to cite one example, is that it is weak where it should be strong and strong where it should be weak.

For example, the president has put his prestige and influence behind a healthcare proposal that a majority of Americans oppose and that *willy nilly* will shift healthcare to the public sector. By contrast, Iran has violated the nonproliferation agreement, has abused its citizens for contesting electoral manipulation, and has been the leading state sponsor of terrorism, yet the president, who should recognize and resist these challenges, seems weak and unresponsive.

The road to serfdom is paved with rights and benefits. People want more of whatever someone else will pay. The casualty in this assessment is personal responsibility and liberty.

We are not yet an authoritarian state and my hope is that America never will be one, but it is imperative we guard against that eventuality recognizing that the rights we invent come with a corresponding withering away of freedom. Big government may not be a problem if it exercises power judiciously and in ways that promote American interests. It is also true, however, that government has a stake in perpetuating itself. It may not always be the problem, but it is rarely the solution, and all the programs that the American people covet may in the end alter the America they once loved and admired.

Now let me comment on the other side of the coin. Despite a breakdown in personal responsibility, a dumbing-down of the population, and defining cultural deviancy down, the United States, with all its flaws and imperfections, is, in my judgment the exceptional nation. A common misperception is that the United States is in decline. In fact, there is a "declinist" school of historical analysis comprised of Dean Koh, Ann Marie Slaughter, Geoffrey Hodgson, Amy Guttman, Richard Sennett, Andrew Bacevich, and Farid Zakaria, among others, who believe in historical inevitability, a Marxist view that the forces of historical determinism are not on our side. However, the biggest mistake any politician can make is to underestimate the people of this great land. I realize things often look bleak and indeed are bleak, but it is important to realize the United States is the land of miracles. We turn detritus into energy; failure into success, and we do it routinely.

I'm reminded, at this moment, of verses from Lee Greenwood's "I'm Proud To Be An American."

"I'm proud to be an American where at least I know I'm free and I won't forget the men who died who gave that right to me."

I've said this before but no matter how many times it is said, it bears repeating: The threats that the United States face from a fanatical Islamic foe are made possible by our devotion to positions that undermine our heritage, accomplishments, and founding.

It is not coincidental that I'm reminded of this condition by the passing of Howard Zinn[1], author of *A People's History of The United States*. This bestselling book, memorialized by the pseudointellectual rants of the actor, Matt Damon, is among the most influential textbooks ever published. Bob Herbert of the *New York Times* wrote a saccharine eulogy that suggested Zinn was a "national treasure." If so, it was a treasure of fool's gold.

Zinn was not a historian in any real sense, but an ideologue who would envision only the blemishes in America's past. For him, the American experiment was predicated on colonialism, imperial aims, exploitation, and enslavement. The curious matter, however, is that Zinn's brand of contemptuous nihilism, his anti-American posture, and hatred of capitalism have caught on among American elites.

Is it any wonder that a multicultural stance that denigrates our national experience and superordinates the goals of other nations is now the prevailing orthodoxy in our schools and colleges? If the United States is the world's exploiter, the despoiler of the environment and the hegemon that restrains the impulse for liberation, why should it be admired? Alas, in many universities, the United States is the enemy. This condition cannot be laid at the doorstep of Mr. Zinn solely, albeit he is a central contributor.

The drumbeat of criticism, however, has taken its toll. Students very often can tell you that Jefferson was a slaveholder, but know nothing about his framing of the Virginia Constitution. According to many, Columbus came to the New World in order to dominate and exploit the indigenous population.

That the United States has been the beacon of hope for mankind, that it has afforded its citizens an unprecedented degree of liberty, and that its openness has yielded technical breakthroughs that have enhanced people across the globe, are conditions that students of an earlier time imbibed as if mother's milk.

That has changed. The pseudosophisticated cynics have come to dominate the academy. American history has been put through the cauldron of political correctness. At best, the United States is merely one of 192 nations with its own history that is neither special nor exceptional; it is simply unique. At worst, American history is a steamy tale of conflict:

workers versus bosses, plantation owners and slaves, guardians of the status quo and change agents.

Many of those who are force-fed these arguments invariably ask logically, "Why should I defend this nation?" If the United States is an outlier whose history infers struggle, the spirit necessary to sustain the nation may not be evident.

I often observe this spiritual enervation; this belief that our time, our glory, has passed. In my judgment that explains, at least in some part, why radical Islamic ideas have gained traction in this nation. How do those who have lost confidence in the national heritage defend against a fanatical faith that has precise goals and direction?

The relentless critics of the nation may not have anticipated this result, but our homegrown radicals invariably express despair with what America stands for, or should I say, what they think America stands for.

Of course, not every American shares this anti-American sentiment, but I am confident a large segment of elitist opinion embraces it. The manifest form it takes varies. There are the cultural warriors who see America as depraved. There are the academics who win plaudits for nihilistic expression (vide: Howard Zinn). There are the radicals ready to leap into anarchy. There are jihadists-homegrown jihadists-who have been radicalized by a faith that preaches triumphalism and a justification for violent behavior.

Our vulnerability does not stem from a lack of resources or even inept leadership, but rather from a void that emanates from not knowing what we believe. Our real enemy is a lack of confidence, of not believing in our own national achievements. Arnold Toynbee argued that civilizations die as a result of suicide, not murder. I am not yet willing to concede death, but there isn't any doubt that America is at risk because of a loss of self-confidence. What ails us internally is at least as threatening as the forces found externally.

Endnotes

Chapter 1. America Agoniste
1 Edward Bellamy, *Looking Backward: 2000-1887*, Massachusetts, Houghton Mcfflin, 1888.
2 Jeane Kirkpatrick, "Dictatorships and Double Standards" *Commentary*, November 1979.
3 Alexander Tyler, The Fall of The Athenian Republic (probably written as a hoax, but nonetheless revealing a great deal about the cycle of democratic development).
4 Oswald Spangler, *The Decline of The West*, NY Oxford Paperbacks, originally published in 1918; Pitrim Sorokin, *The Crisis of Our Age*, New York: Dutton, 1942; Arnold Toynbee, A Study of History, New York: Oxford University Press, 1961.
5 Lawrence v. Texas (2003), Grutter v. Bollinger, Gratz v. Bollinger, 2003.
6 Jean Jacques Rousseau, *The Social Contract*, Translated by G.D.H. Cole, originally published 1762.
7 George Orwell, *1984*, NY, Signet Classics, 1949.
8 William Roepke, *The Economics of A Free Society*, Chicago: Henry Regnery Co., 1963.
9 Richard Neuhaus, *Naked Public Square*, NY: WmB. Eerdmans Publishing, 1984.

Chapter 2. The Age of Experimentation
1 Kathryn Harrison, *Kiss*, NY: Random House, 1997.
2 Franz Kafka, *Metamorphosis*, NY: Tribeca Books, 1915.
3 John Keats, "Party of Lovers", (1795-1821)
4 Betrand Russell, *The Conquest of Happiness*, London: Liveright, 1971.
5 Thomas Harris, *I'm Okay; You're Okay*, NY: Harper and Row, 1967.
6 La Rouchefoucald, "The Moral Maxims of Francis duc de La Rouchefoucald", (1665-1678).
7 "Quotations" G.B. Shaw (1856-1950), 1947.
8 Richard Thaler, Cass Sunstein, *Nudge: Improving Decisions About Health, Wealth and Happiness*, New Haven: Yale U. Press, 2008.
9 Business Insider, "The Enron Curse: Why You Should Avoid Companies That Put Their Name on a Stadium" by Gus Lubin & Simone Foxman, January 18, 2012.

10 Victor Niederhoffer, Laurel Kenner, *Practical Speculation*, NY: John Wiley & Sons, 2005.
11 Oprah's Cut with Martha Stewart, O, *The Oprah Magazine*, August 15, 2000.
12 Francis Fukuyama, "The End of History?" *National Interest*, 1989.
13 Barry Latzer, "The Hollow Core: Failure of the General Education Curriculum," A Report by the American Council of Trustees & Alumni, Washington, DC, April 2004.

Chapter 3. The Slippery Slope of Cultural Degradation
1 "FCC to probe Superbowl halftime" Commission Chey calls Janet Jackson's incident "Classless, crass & deplorable stunt." CNN Money Feb 2, 2004.
2 Thomas Mann, *Magic Mountain* (John Woods, translator) Everyman's Library, 1924.
3 "Boulder library's 'string of penises' artwork miffs some" by Lynn Bartels and Julie Poppen, News Staff Writers, *Rocky Mountain News*, Nov 8, 2001.
4 "Superman: Is 'the American Way' un-pc?" ABC News by Germanm, June 27, 2006.

Chapter 4. False Prophets
1 Salman Rushdie, *Satanic Verses*, N.Y.: Random House Inc., 1988.
2 Dan Brown, *Da Vinci Code*, N.Y.: Vintage Books, 2003.
3 Speth, James Gustave. "The global environment: A program to avoid appalling deterioration." *New York Times* 30 July 2002 http://www.nytimes.com/2002/07/30/opinion/30iht-edspeth_ed3_.html.
4 Speech by Vaclav Klaus at the UN General Assembly Klaus, Václav. Climate Change Conference. United Nations General Assembly. New York. 24 September 2007. Speech.
5 Wigmore, Barry. "Global warming? It's natural, say experts." *DailyMail*. http://www.dailymail.co.uk/news/article-481613/Global-warming-Its-natural-say-experts.html.
6 D.T. Avery, S. Fred Singer, *Unstoppable Global Warming*, MD: Rowman & Littlefield, 2007.

7 Vassilaros, Dimitri. "Calling out Ozone Al." *Tribune Review*. 03 Aug 2007: http://www.pittsburghlive.com/x/pittsburghtrib/s_520391.html.
8 Albert Camus, *The Stranger*, N.Y.: Vintage Books, 1942.

Chapter 5. Technology Is Creating A Brave or Foolish New World
1 Thomas Friedman, *The World is Flat*, N.Y.: Farrar, Straus & Giroux, 2005.
2 The Ghost in the Machine is from British Philosopher Gilbert Ryle's description of Rene Descartes' mind-body dualism.
3 "2003 Civil Literacy Program and Report," Intercollegiate Studies Institute. 2011. http://www.americancivicliteracy.org/2011/conclusion.html.
4 Teddy Roosevelt's letter on January 10, 1917 to Solomon Stanwood Menken, the head of the National Security League and the chairman of its Congress of Constructive Patriotism.

Chapter 6. End of Bipartisanship
1 G. Nunberg, *New York Times*, July 16, 2006.
2 Tom Shales, *Washington Post*, July 23, 2009.
3 John Le Carre, *The Guardian*, November 15, 1997.
4 Quoted in CBC, Podcast, March 21, 2008.
5 Zbigniew Brzezinski, *Second Chance: Three Presidents and The Crisis of American Superpower*, NY: Basic Books, 2007.
6 Paul Krugman, *New York Times*, July 16, 2005.

Chapter 7. Ignorance Is Not Bliss
1 Ben Wattenberg, The *Good News Is, The Bad News Is Wrong*, NY: Touchstone Books, 1984.
2 Paul Ehrlich, *The Population Bomb*, Sierra Club/Ballatine Books, 1968.
3 John Ferejohn, Gattail Voting in Recent Presidential Elections, *American Political Science Review*, June 1983.
4 Ilya Somia quoted in Tom McDonald, U.S. Elections Decided by Know-Nothings, Grassroot Institute of Hawaii, February 6, 2007.
5 Quoted in Jon Blackwell, *The Trentonian* "1935: The Poll That Took America's Pulse," 1936.

6 Molly Ivins, "The Uncompassionate Conservative" *Mother Jones,* November/December 2003
7 Sandip Roy, Pacific News Service, November 2, 2009.
8 James Donahue, "Yes World, American Voters Are Really Dumb," *Daily Mirror,* November 3, 2004.
9 Barack Obama, *Dreams of My Father: A Story of Race and Inheritance,* Times Books, 1995.

Chapter 8. Things Fall Apart
1 Sun Tzu, *Art of War,* NY: Dover Books, 1971, (originally published about 500 B.C.).
2 Carl Von Clauswitz, Principles of War, The Military Service Publishing Co, 1942 (originally published in 1812.)
3 David Brooks, *Bobos in Paradise: The New Upper Class and How They Got There,* NY: Simon and Schuster, 2000.
4 Daniel Bell, *The Cultural Contradictions of Capitalism,* NY: Basic Books, 1976.
5 "Edward Said and The Possibilities of Humanism", R. Radhakrishman in *A Legacy of Emancipation and Representation,* edited by Adel Iskander and Hakem Rustom, U. of California Press, 2010.
6 Quoted in *Institute for Historical Review,* July 16, 2004.
7 David Bauder, "Peter Arnett Fired," *MilitaryCity.com,* 2003.
8 Blair Goldstein, "Soros on Bush, Iraq and Unchecked Power," *Independent,* February 25, 2004.
9 George Soros, *Age of Fallibility: Consequences of The War on Terror,* NY: Public Affairs Books, 2006.
10 George Soros, "On Israel, America and AIPAC," *New York Review of Books,* May 10, 2007.

Epilogue
1 Howard Zinn, *A People's History of The U.S.,* NY: Harper Collins, 1980.

Index

1960 presidential election, 117
1984, 18, 28
2000 presidential election, 118
2004 presidential election, 117–21
2008 presidential election, 122–26
2009 as transformational year, 10

A
Adams, Lorraine, 69–71
affirmative action, 24
The Age of Fallibility, 158
air pollution, 72
Allen, Frederick Lewis, 11
Allen, George, 147
al Qaeda, 8, 107, 112, 157
America
    the "idea" of, 138–40
    vision of, 50–51
America Agonistes, 13–30
American Academy of Pediatrics, 54
American Beauty, 33
American business in 2010, 14
American Council of Trustees and Alumni, 50
American Firsters, 144
American flag display refused, 60, 61
American International Group, 14
American public lacks knowledge, 113–14
An Inconvenient Truth, 74
anonymity, loss of, 81–82
ANSWER (Act Now to Stop War and End Racism), 102, 159
"anti-art," 34
anti-Semitism, 148
anti-war protesters, 159–60
Arbour, Louise, 105
"A Republic, if you can keep it," 20
Arnett, Peter, 154
"art" of Andrea Fraser, 59–61
authoritarian regimes, 19
avatars of moral equivalence (AME), 150–51
Avery, Dennis, 73–74
Ayers, Bill, 125

B
"Back to Basics" (BTB), 31
Baker, Jim, 120
Baseball Hall of Fame, 96–97
behavioral targeting, 80
Bell, Daniel, 141
Bellamy, Edward, 13
Benedict XVI, Pope, 104
bias in reporting, 92
bipartisanship, end of, 91–111
Bobos in Paradise, 138
Boeing aircraft, 80
Bolton, John, 111, 157–58
Bork, Robert, 111
Brooks, David, 138
Brown, Dan, 70
Brown, Janice Rogers, 100
Browning, 29
Brzezinski, Zbigniew, 109
Buchanan, Pat, 105, 144
Buckley, William, 33
Bull Durham, 96–97
Bush, George W., 42

approval rating of, 115–17
reputation of, 10
and war on terrorism, 8

C
Cameron, Dan, 60
Camus, Albert, 78
capitalism, characteristics of, 141–42
carbon dioxide, 72
carbon footprint, 37
Carter, Jimmy, 42
CBS and wardrobe malfunction, 55–57
ceramic penises as art, 61, 62
Chambers, John, 45
change, discussion of, 15
Chase, Chevy, 94
child care centers, 17
China Syndrome, 44
The Chronicle of Higher Education, 43
Chrysler Corporation, 14
Churchill, Winston, 116
CIA tactics, and terrorism, 8
Citicorp, 14
civic literacy, 85–87
civilization, historians of, 22
civil libertarians, 26
civil religion, reemergence of, 50
Civil Rights Act of 1964, 24
"civil rights leaders," 17
Clark, Ramsey, 102, 144, 154, 159
Clinton, Hillary, 99, 121
as radical secularist, 124
Clinton, William, 42
comedians and political commentary, 93

community leaders or gang members, 92
Community Reinvestment Act, 8–9, 134
compassionate conservatism, 134
Constitutional Convention, 20
The Country Chronicle, 15
courtship, and how practices have changed, 16
credit market in America, 47–48
credit meltdown of 2008, 9
crisis tactic, 129–30
criticism, drumbeat of, 163
Cronkite, Walter, 68–69
The Cultural Contradictions of Capitalism, 141
cultural decline in the United States, 15–16
cultural degradation, 52–67, 83–84
cultural revolution, as abandonment of tradition, 33
cultural vitality, sustaining, 50
culture war, 138–39
current events, lack of knowledge about, 83–84

D
Daily Mirror (London), 119
DaVinci Code, 70
The Day After Tomorrow, 95
declinism, 9, 11, 162
Demme, Jonathan, 95
democracy, discussion of, 23
democracy or republic, 19
Democratic Party, and anti-American posture, 106
Descartes, 81

Desperate Housewives, 33, 42
diets, fad, 31
diversity
    present definition of, 17
    term, 26
divorce rate in America, 39
documentaries as political
    diatribes, 96
Dohrn, Bernadette, 125
Do It!, 28
Dougherty, Mike, 66
Dowd, Maureen, 98
Dreams of My Father, 124
dress, recent change in, 16
drug abuse, 41–42
drug culture, 63–64
drug use and party in power, 41–42
"dumbing down," 83–84

E
editorials or news reports, 91
education
    on continual trial, 31–32
    and self-esteem campaign, 38
Ehrlich, Paul, 113
Einstein, Albert, 28
Eliot, Charles, 86
Emanuel, Rahm, 129
Ender, Chris, 57
"End of History," 11, 47
entertainers
    and political bias, 93
entertainment, and its role in our
    culture, 53
environment, preservation of, 72–73
equal opportunity confused with
    equal results, 24

equal protection under the law,
    24–25
establishment clause, 29–30
evil, face of, 152
excrement as art, 60
experimentation, age of, 31–51

F
Fahrenheit 9/11, 96, 115
false prophets, 68–79
fame/infamy, 26
family, decline of traditional,
    39–41
fatalism, 49–50
FCC regulation of TV, 56
feelings, discussion of, 35–36
Ferejohn, John, 114
Fifth Column, 107
First Amendment, 29, 93, 96, 149
Fish, Stanley, 152–53
food tastes, change in, 16
foreign policy
    in 2000, 7
    of apology, 10, 155–56
    of Colin Powell, 17–18
    of Obama, 122, 128
Fortas, Abe, 111
Fourteenth Amendment, 24
"Fourth Awakening," 30
Franco-American relations,
    155–56
Franklin, Benjamin, 20
Fraser, Andrea, 59–60
freedom fighters or terrorists, 152
freedom of association, 141
free market economy, 28
free speech, 141

Freidan, Betty, 105
Friedman, Thomas, 80
Fukuyama, Francis, 11, 47

G
gambling, 64–65
gang members or community leaders, 92
Garafalo, Janeane, 75, 87
gender politics, 40
General Motors, in 1960 and 2010, 14
"ghost in the machine," 81
Gill, A. A., 98
Gingrich, Newt, 120
Ginsberg, Ruth Bader, 100
Giuliani, Rudolph, 20
Global 2000 Report, 71
globalization of the Internet, 81
The Good News Is The Bad News Is Wrong, 112
Google, 80
Gore, Al, 37, 73–74
government ownership of business, 10
Gralapp, Marcelee, 61, 62
Gramsci, Antonio, 34, 126–28, 146
Greenwood, Lee, 162
Griffin, Robert, 111
Guantanamo, coverage of, 103

H
Hale, Nathan, 137
happiness, 38–39
Hardball, 97
Harris, Dan, 66
Harvard seniors and freshmen, 86
healthcare
　under government control, 14
　as primary issue, 52
Hearst, William Randolph, 148
Heartland Institute, 73, 74
Herbert, Bob, 75, 163
heroes, flawed public, 68
Hilton, Paris, 85
historians of civilization, 22
history
　is cyclical, 52
　and world economy, 47
Hoffman, Abbie, 28
Hollings, Ernest, 147–48
"The Hollow Core," 50
Hollywood
　and political innuendo, 93
　and politics, 93, 95–96
hubris, 45–48
humanitarian, meaning of, 18
"Hung Out To Dry," 61, 62
Hussein, Saddam, 144–45, 148, 154
hypocrisy, 19

I
"Idomeneo," 103
Iliad, 34
illegitimacy rate among teenagers, 55
immigration bill, and rights, 21–22
"I'm Okay, You're Okay," 38
I'm Proud To Be An American, 162
Imus, Don, 36
income disparity, 112
infamy/fame, 26

Intelligence Identities Protection Act, 110
Intercollegiate Studies Institute (ISI), 85
Internal Revenue Service, 18
Iowans
    on issues, 87
    on president's performance, 88
    and Washington bureaucracy, 88
Iraq War, 144-48
    America divided on, 48-49
    media coverage of, 112
    opposition/support, 115-17
    opposition to, 153-57
Islamic terrorism, 7
Islamists, radical, 149-51
Islamophobia, 149-50
Israel
    and Jewish vote, 147
    and Palestine, 158
Ivins, Molly, 119

J
Jackson, Janet, 33, 55-57
Jackson, Jesse, 17, 76
Jackson, Michael, 68-69
Jefferson, Thomas, 113
    and religion, 29
The Jewel of Medina, 69-71
Johnson, Lyndon, 46-47
Jones, Sherry, 69-71
journalism, bias in, 92
Judeo-Christian principles, 13, 24-25

Jylands-Posten cartoons, 104

K
Kafka, Franz, 34
Keats, 35
Kennedy, Ted, 68-69
Kenner, Laurel, 45
Kenobi, Obi-Wan, 36
Kerry, John, 119
Kettle, John, 23
Keynes, John Maynard, 10
Kimball, Roger, 44
Kim Jong-Il, 129
King, Rodney, 92
Kirkpatrick, Jeane, 19
Kiss, 33
Klaus, Vaclav, 73
"know nothings," 114
Kopechne, Mary Jo, 68
Kraft Foods, and ads for junk food, 53-55
Krauthammer, Charles, 11, 148
Krugman, Paul, 110

L
La Rochefoucauld, 19, 39
Last Temptation of Christ, 70
Lay, Kenneth, 45
"Leave It To Beaver" mom, 32
Le Carré, John, 105
Lee, Ang, 62-63
leftist policy prescriptions, 160
Leno, Jay, 20, 53, 83-85
liberal, meaning of, 19
liberalism, 140
    encroachment of, 21

libertarian paternalism, 43–44
Lieberman, Joe, 106
Limbaugh, Rush, 91
Lincoln, Abraham, 50
Lindberg, Charles, 144
Little Red school, 101–2
Looking Backward, 13

M
Magic Mountain, 59
The Manchurian Candidate remake, 95
Mann, Thomas, 59
Manzoni, Piero, 60
market, free, 43–44
marriage, 39–40
Marxism, 47
Matthews, Chris, 97
McCain, John, 122
McCall, Carl, 75
McClellan, Ian, 34
media bias, 91–92
media coverage of Iraq War, 112
Media Research Center, 103
"The Media *vs.* The War on Terror," 103
Meeropol, Robert, 101–2
Mellencamp, John, 94
military readiness, 143–45
Mohammed, Khalid Sheikh, 10
Mohammed, Prophet, 69–71
    cartoons in *Jylands-Posten,* 104
Moncton, Lord, 73–74
Moore, Michael, 91, 106, 114, 115
morals, public, 42
mortgages
    government-subsidized, 8–9
    uncollateralized, 47–48
multiculturalism, present definition of, 17
Munich Accord, 89
Muslim Brotherhood, 108
Muslims, sensitivity to, 136

N
Naked Public Square, 29
national principles, consensus needed, 26
Neuenfel, Hans, 103
Neuhaus, Richard, 29
"new journalism," 91
news, bad/good, 112–37
news reports or editorials, 91
new world, brave or foolish?, 80–90
New York Times, and term "protesters," 18
Niederhoffer, Victor, 45
Nudge: Improving Decisions About Health, Wealth and Happiness, 43–44
Nunberg, Geoffrey, 91, 92

O
"oasis strategy," 34
Obama, Barack
    as first black president, 77
    foreign policy of, 78, 122, 128
    and Franco-American relations, 76, 77
    as a man apart, 78, 79
    and the Messiah syndrome, 98–99
    presidential campaign of 2008, 9–10

and spreading the wealth, 10
Obama administration actions, 133–35
O'Connor, Sandra Day, 25
Ofili, Chris, 60
"only in America," 136
Only Yesterday and Since Yesterday, 11
Organization of the Islamic Conference, 105
Orwell, George, 17, 18

P
Paige (Sec. of Education), 31
Palestine, and Israel, 158
Palin, Sarah, 123, 124–25
paternalism, 43–44
Patriot Act, 8
Pelosi, Nancy, 121
A People's History of the United States, 163
Perle, Richard, 148
Petroskey, Dale, 96
Plame, Valerie, 109
Policy Planning Group, 127
political commentary by comedians, 93
political images in Hollywood, 42
political propaganda rating system, 93–94
politicians, and moral principles, 42
politics and public's lack of knowledge of, 114–15
The Population Bomb, 113
pornography, 19–20
    is ubiquitous, 33, 56
"Post Yesterday," 11
Potemkin, Mandy, 93
Powell, Colin
    foreign policy of, 17–18
    and Iraq war, 8
Powell, Michael, 56
preemptive conciliation, 10
presidential campaign of 2008, 9–10
privacy, loss of, 81–82
"privacy notion," 25
prophets, false, 68–79
protesters, term, 18
psychology, reevaluation of, 32
pursuit of happiness, 38–39

R
race, issue of, 24–25
race/ethnicity, 13
Radosh, Ronald, 101–2
Ramadan, Tariq, 108
Random House publishers, 70
Rangel, Charlie, 76
rebellion as expression of feelings, 36
redlining made illegal, 9
religion, 27–28, 29–30
    freedom of, 149
religious tolerance, 136–37
rent control (NYC), 20
republican form of government, 20–21
Republicans
    and morality, 42–43
    political strategy of, 135
republic or democracy, 19
Revkin, Andrew, 37

Rice, Susan, 127
Rich, Frank, 33, 106–7
rights
    contemporary, 21
    discussion of, 21–22
Robbins, Tim, 96–97
Roberts, John, 99–100
rock stars and pornography, 56–58
Roepke, Wilhelm, 28
Rooney, Andy, 56
Roosevelt, Franklin, 102
Roosevelt, Teddy, 89, 90
Rosenberg Fund for Children, 101
Rousseau, Jean Jacques, 27–28
Rove, Karl, 93, 109–11
Roy, Sandip, 119
Rumsfeld, Donald, 120
Rushdie, Salman, 105
Russell, Bertrand, 38

S

Said, Edward, 146, 152
Salafist leader on life/death, 8
Satanic Verses, 105
SAT scores in decline, 14
Schlesinger, Arthur, 99
Schumer, Chuck, 99–100, 110
SDS protests in 1960s, 13
Second Chance, 109
secularism, 27–28
secularist position, 124
self-esteem campaign in education, 38
Selleck, Tom, 97
"Sensation" exhibit, 60
sentimentality, fake, 36–38

September 11, 2001 attacks, 7, 153
sex on television, 54
sexual encounter as "art," 59–61
sexual initiation, early, 54–55
Shales, Tom, 99
Sharpton, Al, 17, 76
Shaw, George Bernard, 39
Sheen, Martin, 97
Simmons, Gene, 57
"The Simple Life," 85
Singer, Fred, 73
Slaughter, Anne Marie, 127
Smith, Adam, 28
social integration, as American aim, 26
Somin, Ilya, 114
Sorokin, Pitirim, 22, 49, 52
Soros, George, 119, 157–58
Sotomayor, Sonia, 13
"Spelling Bee," 93
Spengler, 22
Speth, James Gustave, 71–72
spreading the wealth, 10
Stewart, Martha, 46
stimulus package, 129
The Stranger, 78
Streisand, Barbra, 94
Sunshine, Cass, 43–44
Superman, 66–67
Supreme Court
    decisions, 24–25, 29, 87, 138
    justices, 13, 99–100, 111

T

Taking Woodstock, 62–63
technology, 80–90

television, 32–33
　ads to kids, 53–54
　and pornography, 55–58
　programming and cultural
　　degradation, 55–56
Tenebaum, Inez, 148
terrorists
　or freedom fighters, 152
　as victims, 103
"Texas Bandito," 94
Thaler, Richard, 43–44
threats, probable/unlikely, 44
Timberlake, Justin, 55, 56
Tocqueville, and religion, 29
totalitarian regimes, 19
Toynbee, Arnold, 22, 164
tradition, abandonment of, 33
transformational America, 11
transformational year 2009, 10
transnational progressivism, 9
Tyler, Alexander, 22–23

U
Ugly American, 155–57
unhappiness as inspiration,
　38–39
Universal Health Care, 128
Unstoppable Global Warming, 73

V
van Gogh, Theo, 104, 142
Veblen, Thorstein, 86
VH1, on rock stars and
　pornography, 57
Virginia Tech murders, 36

virtual manufacturing, 80
voting irregularities, 117–18

W
Walker, Jimmy, 55
Wall Street greed, 48
Walters, John, 41
war
　as necessary, 143–45
　protest (1960s), 13
　and resistors, 146
　against terrorism, 7
　theories of, 138
wardrobe malfunction, 33, 55–57
Wattenberg, Ben, 112
Wealth of Nations, 28
Webster, Daniel, 69
Wedding Crashers, 93, 95
"we the people," 21
Wilson, Joseph, 109
Wolfe, Tom, 42
Wolfowitz, Paul, 148
Woodstock, 62–64
　another view of, 63
　generation of, 25
words
　changed meanings of, 15–16
　to influence opinion, 18–19
world economy, 47
World Trade Center, 7, 50, 134,
　138, 152–53
Wright, Rev., 125

Z
Zinn, Howard, 163